Praise for
Surrender All

"Joni Lamb proves that surrendering all to the Lord ultimately results in unlimited happiness, peace, health, joy, success, and love beyond all comprehension. *Surrender All* is inspirational! A blessing! A must-read!"

—GAVIN MACLEOD, actor and author of *Back on Course*

"Joni Lamb speaks to the heart. Her uplifting, motivating message will show you just how simple and powerful surrender to God is—how surrender can turn hopelessness to purpose and helplessness to power. By surrendering all, your doubts will be replaced by confidence, your fears diminished by strength, and your desires turned to dreams-that-can-come-true."

—BISHOP T. D. JAKES, senior pastor, The Potter's House, Dallas

"*Surrender All* is a book to be savored and saved. During a trying time in my life, Joni's words and the stories blessed me and reminded me that I can trust the Lord with everything. I can continue to cling to Proverbs 3:5–6. I know this book will greatly encourage everyone who reads it, and I hope thousands will!"

—FRANCINE RIVERS, author of *Redeeming Love*

"Joni Lamb writes with believable truth and testimony, ignited by the fact that she has learned and lives out the message she delivers here—*Surrender All!*"

—JACK W. HAYFORD, president, The International Foursquare Church and chancellor, The King's Seminary

SURRENDER All

SURRENDER *All*

YOUR ANSWER *to* LIVING
with PEACE,
POWER & PURPOSE

JONI LAMB

WATERBROOK
PRESS

SURRENDER ALL
PUBLISHED BY WATERBROOK PRESS
12265 Oracle Boulevard, Suite 200
Colorado Springs, Colorado 80921
A division of Random House Inc.

All Scripture quotations, unless otherwise indicated, are taken from the New King James Version®. Copyright © 1982 by Thomas Nelson Inc. Used by permission. All rights reserved. Scripture quotations marked (KJV) are taken from the King James Version. Scripture quotations marked (NIV) are taken from the Holy Bible, New International Version®. NIV®. Copyright © 1973, 1978, 1984 by International Bible Society. Used by permission of Zondervan Publishing House. All rights reserved.

Details in some anecdotes and stories have been changed to protect the identities of the persons involved. All personal stories used by permission.

ISBN 978-1-4000-7375-7

Published in the United States by WaterBrook Multnomah, an imprint of The Doubleday Publishing Group, a division of Random House Inc., New York.

WATERBROOK and its deer colophon are registered trademarks of Random House Inc.

Library of Congress Cataloging-in-Publication Data
Lamb, Joni.
    Surrender all : your answer to living with peace, power & purpose / Joni Lamb.—1st ed.
      p. cm.
    Includes bibliographical references.
    ISBN 978-1-4000-7375-7
    1. Submissiveness—Religious aspects—Christianity. 2. Control (Psychology)—Religious aspects—Christianity. 3. Christian life. I. Title.
BV4647.A25L36 2008
248.4—dc22

                                                                2008017949

Printed in the United States of America

2009

10 9 8 7 6 5 4 3 2

SPECIAL SALES
Most WaterBrook Multnomah books are available in special quantity discounts when purchased in bulk by corporations, organizations, and special-interest groups. Custom imprinting or excerpting can also be done to fit special needs. For information, please e-mail SpecialMarkets@WaterBrookMultnomah.com or call 1-800-603-7051.

Television personality **Joni Lamb** is executive producer and host of the daily *JONI* show, a talk show on Daystar Television, which earned the National Religious Broadcasters Talk Show of the Year award in 2004.

A lively and sometimes unpredictable half-hour talk show, broadcast twice a day, the *JONI* show covers a wide range of relevant issues, controversial subjects, and hard-hitting news topics with candor and wit. It features life-changing testimonies and expert opinions, an array of notable guests, and a fresh perspective on issues ranging from health and nutrition to divorce and raising children. The show reaches a broad, multicultural audience that transcends denomination and race by focusing on the importance and relevance of the gospel in today's society.

Joni and her husband, Marcus Lamb, president/CEO of Daystar Television Network, built and founded Daystar, which owns more than fifty television stations, reaches approximately 75 million homes in the U.S., and goes into every country of the world.

The Lambs live in Dallas, Texas, and are the parents of three children: Jonathan, Rachel, and Rebecca. Their family ministers frequently throughout the country.

Contents

Foreword

*J*oni Lamb is a remarkable woman! Many of you know this from seeing her on television. But did you know that one of the remarkable things about her is that "what you see, is what you get"? The way Joni is on television is the way she is at home, at the grocery store, at the service station, and at a ball game, and that is one of her charms. She is genuine—and she is as beautiful on the inside as she is on the outside.

I know because I've been blessed to be married to her for twenty-five incredible years. And I'm more in love with her today than ever. Though at times our journey has been difficult, Joni and I have both learned to surrender. And that's what drove Joni to write this book. You see, it wasn't Joni's idea to write a book, especially about herself. She was asked to do this. After praying, God spoke to her heart: *Surrender.*

That one word is truly the story of her life. Again, I know because I have been right there with her every step of the way. Joni and I are strong believers in destiny and purpose. If we weren't, there wouldn't be a Daystar Television Network reaching millions of people around the world! We know that God does have a plan and a purpose for your life. You have only to surrender to Him to see His best plan fulfilled in your life.

In this book, Joni will give you many examples of how to surrender—examples from her own life and the lives of the many others she's interviewed on television. (True to her nature, Joni doesn't keep the book just about herself, but allows many other wonderful people to be shared as well.) These are true life stories, and you will identify with many of them. You will laugh and cry and rejoice—and you will be inspired to apply many of the lessons learned to your own life. You also will want to share this book with family and friends and refer back to many of its stories again and again.

For now, sit back, get comfortable, grab a pillow, a cup of coffee, and some tissues and get ready to go on a ride of adventure as Joni Lamb leads you down the road of surrender. At the end of the road, you will find God's best plan for you—and you will not be disappointed!

Marcus D. Lamb, founder and president

Daystar Television Network

Dallas, Texas

Preface

I was six years old when I first became aware of God's presence. My friend Laurie Pierce and I were playing at her house a few miles from mine in Greenville, South Carolina. We were in her wooded backyard, on the swing set. I don't remember what Laurie said or did that made me angry, but I responded by pushing my best friend off her swing. She fell hard and ran to the house crying. I stood there feeling guilty and afraid until Laurie's mother came outside and knelt down beside me.

"Did you push Laurie off the swing?" she asked.

I stared at the ground where my toe was making little circles in the dirt.

"Now, Joni, I wasn't out here to see what happened, but *you* know what happened. And there is someone else who also knows what happened because He sees everything," she said. "So let's just pray and ask Him about it."

Immediately I experienced, for the very first time, an overwhelming sensation and realization of God's presence. I comprehended His omnipresence and omniscience. And I grasped the fact that I was accountable to Him.

"I did it," I said to Laurie's mother—then promptly started crying, not so much in fear as in gratitude for the wonderful gift she had given me.

Laurie's mother sat on one of the swings and pulled me into a gentle hug. She shared with me the story of Jesus, the Son of God. Best of all, she told me that He loved me. I grew up in a Christian family, so I had heard of God's love before; but on that day, the truth of those words resonated in my young brain, my consciousness, and my soul.

Laurie's mother must have sensed that something spiritual and pro-found had occurred. "Let's pray and ask Jesus to forgive you," she said.

That prayer marked my first step in the lifelong process of surrender-ing in every aspect of my life to Jesus, the Son of God. I was instilled with a reverential fear of God. I realized that God loved me, but He was also aware of my every action and my every thought. I realized that if I did something hurtful, I not only disappointed Him, I hurt Him.

Surrendering control of my life to my Creator began as an act of rev-erence, but it resulted in exciting joy and wonderful comfort. From my ear-liest realization of God's existence, to my full surrender to God at age twenty, to my continued walk with the Holy Spirit now as a middle-aged woman, I have placed my life in the Lord's hands.

I share my story and the stories of others who have surrendered to the Lord in hopes that you will grasp the simple yet profound importance of surrendering your life to the One who created us all. Surrender doesn't guarantee a worry-free life. We are still faced with struggles and trials along with our daily victories and moments of great hope. My desire, most of all, is to help you find your place in a world full of chaos and human suffer-ing. There is a place of peace, power, and purpose in this world—and it be-gins with one word. *Surrender.*

Introduction

The desert surrounding the holy city of Jerusalem seems like a romantic place to get a call from God, but it's not as glamorous as it sounds. The ground is hard and unforgiving, full of deep and deadly crevices, as if a giant creature had carved the land with massive fingernails to trap unsuspecting travelers—much like the Path of Surrender we followed to obey that call. But here is where my husband, Marcus, and I began the journey that brought us through "crevices" deeper than any we saw in the Sinai Desert as we traveled through Egypt.

We had only been in the Bedouin region for a short time, when Marcus noticed something unusual: a satellite antenna poked up from the top of each tent in this dry and barren landscape. It seemed incongruous, this modern technology in so simple and harsh a land. Marcus realized that God had been planting a vision in his heart and mind, telling him that television is a tool for spreading the Lord's teachings to a vast audience—anywhere in the world, day and night.

God had come up with a very tall order for us in the Holy Land. At that point, in March 1983, we were newly married. We were on the road constantly, preaching and ministering with revivals in twenty states. We knew nothing about operating a television station, Christian or otherwise. So when the Lord spoke to Marcus while he was standing on the Mount of Olives in Jerusalem about moving to Montgomery, Alabama, he said three things to God.

1. *Why would You ask me to stop doing something You were blessing—evangelism!—in order to go and build a Christian TV station?*

2. *Lord, I don't know how to build a Christian TV station.*

3. *Lord, I don't have a million dollars to build a Christian TV station!*

You might think that God would respond with a lengthy dialogue to answer all those questions after giving Marcus such a tall order. But all He did was repeat the assignment: *Go to Montgomery and build a Christian television station.*

Marcus and I were excited by this, but we were also flustered and more than a little clueless about how to get started. We puzzled over it for several months. Then, in the fall of 1983, Marcus decided that we needed to seriously focus on it. He suggested that we go on a three-day fast to make sure we were clear on what the Lord wanted us to do.

Like most other women, I'd done my share of dieting, even back when I really didn't need to diet. But I'd never gone on a three-day fast where you didn't eat even a carrot stick or a bran muffin. Let me tell you, it is no walk in the park. I thought I was going to die! After the first day, the headaches were excruciating. But we both persevered through prayer, and when it was over, Marcus felt the Lord had made it very clear that we were to find a way to start a Christian television station.

By the following January, we were in Montgomery.

Risking All

A few years before, Marcus had been helping a Montgomery minister in his efforts to build a television station—long before we had any thoughts of doing it ourselves. This minister, whom Marcus and I had preached for, had gotten a permit for a broadcast license. He'd raised quite a bit of money, but the Federal Communications Commission sets a time limit when it issues permits, and the funds weren't coming in fast enough for him to make the deadline. If you don't build your station within the allotted time, you lose your permit. Our friend was facing that predicament, so he'd decided to sell his permit.

Again, at that point, we were ministering around the country and not at all thinking about starting a television station. So Marcus had helped our Montgomery friend sell his permit to another group of Christians we knew from Kentucky who'd been looking for a broadcast license. It was strange because Marcus kept getting pulled back into this deal, investing money into the project, even though he wasn't part of the ownership. It was as if we were being prepared for a role that we could not foresee.

As it turned out, the Kentucky group couldn't get their deal put together to build a station in Montgomery. By the time they went looking for a buyer, God had clued us in on His plan for us. Suddenly, we were ready to take on the mission ourselves. We entered into an agreement to buy the Montgomery permit. The FCC gave us the same deadline, which was about eighteen months, to get the station up and running.

We gave it our best shot, but we were a couple of newlywed evangelists, still in our twenties. We weren't venture capitalists. Neither of us even knew what venture capitalists were. Back then, we'd seen our share of church bake sales, but we'd never had to raise such serious capital. Initially we borrowed money from family members. We borrowed against our home. We took money out of savings and sold investments. I'm not sure, but Marcus may have taken a paper route and sold lemonade on street corners, trying to make it happen. As the deadline approached, the vultures were circling. Other groups were trying to buy the permit out from under us because they didn't think we could pull it off. And we had doubts about it too.

We'd surrendered it to God and did the best we could to follow His plan for us, but as that deadline loomed it sure seemed like we were going to come up short. Marcus told me we were running out of time and money. Finally one day in exasperation he asked me: "Joni, are you willing to lose all that we have and everything our friends and family have given us because we believe God wants us to build this Christian television station?"

I was still new at the wife thing, but I stood by my man as best as I could, and I really believed we had a mandate from God as well. "Whatever you think we should do, Marcus, I'm with you," I said. At that point, we realized that we could lose everything, but we were willing to take that risk because we knew God had spoken to us.

Marcus felt God had called us to start this Christian station in Montgomery and that we had to do whatever it took to fulfill that mission. "The money belongs to Him, not us. And if I have to work a secular job the rest of my life to pay it back, I'm willing to do that," he said.

And so we surrendered our finances to the Lord. We risked it all, and we very easily could have lost it all.

Community Effort

As a first grader, Marcus got fifty cents a week for allowance, which covered his recess Popsicle habit since they were only ten cents back then. But then Marcus learned about tithing 10 percent, which meant that he should give a nickel to the collection box at church. He did the math and figured he'd be a nickel short one day a week at Popsicle time. It was one of his first big challenges of faith. Did he tithe or did he keep the nickel so he could continue having a Popsicle at recess every day?

"Even as a little boy, the Devil tried to challenge me about finances," Marcus says. "He said that a nickel wouldn't make any difference to our church. The Devil tried to reason that it probably cost the church five cents just to provide an envelope for the tithe. But I put God first then and I always have, especially when it comes to finances."

Marcus and I have seen, both in our personal finances and in the ministry's finances, that if we put God first and surrender our finances to the Lord, then He will take care of us. And God was certainly working on our behalf once we surrendered our finances to Him. A miracle occurred. When we fully committed ourselves to God's will, others invested in that commitment with their own money.

One Sunday afternoon, a man drove by and saw the bumper sticker on our car that said WMCF-TV "45 Alive!" We couldn't have felt more that the opposite—"45 Dead!"—was true. Curious what "45 Alive!" was about, the man stopped and came into our studio to see what we were doing. I was seven months pregnant with our first child, pushing Marcus around on double-decker scaffolding so he could work on raising the drop ceiling for TV lights. Our landlord had the air conditioning turned off to save money, even though it was summer and more than 100 degrees in the room. Seeing our dedication and realizing we were working in this hot building all alone, this man's heart was touched. He wrote a check for $1,000, and said he would be back the next morning with his pickup truck and tools to help us do the work. We were like little kids building a tree house out of scrap lumber, but eventually others caught the vision for Christian television and joined in to help us.

We built our first television station with borrowed money, baling wire, duct tape, and papier-mâché. I'm serious about that. We got the station up and running and on the air thanks largely to the fact that two other local stations were updating their equipment. They were throwing out all of their old electronics, including a transmitter made for black-and-white television that was being sent to the dump. Whatever they put on the curb, including that transmitter, we took. We had three cameras that looked like they'd been part of Dr. Frankenstein's laboratory; our castoff transmitter was the oldest model in the country. I'm surprised it didn't have a hand-crank starter.

But we had the Lord on our broadcast team. His plan—and a whole lot of duct tape and silicone—got WMCF-TV 45 on the air on October 12, 1985, as the first full-power Christian television station ever built in Alabama. Someone told us we were the youngest couple ever to build a television station in the United States, but we knew better. We knew that it was the Lord's station and the result of His work through us and the many, many other people who pitched in with their money, skills, time, prayers, and support.

Personal Cost

Even though Marcus and I believed our new television station was God's plan, that didn't mean God stepped in and made every production something heavenly. We were definitely Christian broadcasters-in-training for a long, long time. Once the station was on the air, we somehow kept it going, but it was amateur hour. And it wasn't always pretty to watch. Our part-time accountant made a mistake and our check to the power company bounced—so the studio's electricity was cut off during one show. Our three very old rummage sale cameras had lenses that somehow made Marcus's eyes look like a raccoon's. It may have been an act of God when all three cameras blew up on the same day.

While we were struggling to get our seat-of-the-pants Christian broadcast operation going with only one paid engineer and a bunch of volunteers, we didn't have any income to speak of, so we had to surrender our personal financial situation to God too. We needed a second car for Marcus, so he bought an old rust-bucket Datsun for $400. (There was no extra charge for the hole in the floorboard.) The car was such a junker that its engine once burst into flames while he was driving it on the highway.

Our vehicles and broadcast equipment weren't the only problems in the early days of WMCF-TV. When I first started appearing on the air with Marcus, I was so nervous I'd get nauseous before every show and my mouth would dry up so much that I could hardly talk. As a result I didn't say much at first. Finally, one afternoon when I was getting ready, the Holy Spirit said, "Just go and be yourself, and I'll go with you. I'll tell you what to say and even give you the questions to ask." I still follow His guidance today. I am totally dependent on Him. He has been my teacher, and we've been working together ever since.

Thanks to another blessing, I also became quite adept at multitasking at our first television station. Our son Jonathan was born in the early days of WMCF-TV, and I often kept him in a baby carrier just off the studio set after I joined Marcus on the air. If Jonathan started crying, I would walk off the set, feed him, rock him to sleep, or change his diaper. God showed us that we had to nurture, love, and protect our newborn TV station just like our newborn son, who was born October 19, 1985, seven days afer we first went on the air.

Of course, just as we began to feel as if we knew what we were doing in Montgomery, the Lord came a-knocking with a new plan for us. He began to deal with Marcus about going to Dallas and acquiring a broadcast license there, which set off a bit of a mad scramble as we tried to figure out how to pull off that new mission. God's goal for us was to reach ten times as many people with the good news of the gospel. We couldn't see how to accomplish that while also keeping the station in Montgomery, so we decided to sell WMCF.

It quickly became apparent that the wisest money move would be to sell the station to one of the secular groups bidding to buy it from us for big sums of cash so they could turn it into a network affiliate. We could have justified that move easily enough by saying that the additional dollars from the sale would give us more funds to reach a bigger audience in Dallas. But God let Marcus know that He wanted the Montgomery station to remain a voice for Christian broadcasting. He told Marcus that even if we sell our station to a Christian group for less money that He would make up for every lost dollar after we got to Dallas. In 1990 we sold the Montgomery station for just the debt owed on it, ensuring that it would continue to broadcast Christian content twenty-four hours a day just as God wanted. Basically, we sold that station for about one fourth of what we could have gotten from a secular group.

But the biggest act of financial surrender came in the fact that we had to sign a no-compete clause with the buyers. The deal demanded that for at least five years we could not have a program on television or build another Christian television station within a hundred miles. That was a great surrender because we had been doing the daily program in Montgomery for almost seven years. People had watched our children and our ministry grow up over that time.

We were torn about giving up the daily ministry program and television station in order to follow the Lord's plan in Dallas. Marcus said he felt like

King Solomon confronted with the two women who both claimed the baby was theirs. But the true mother was willing to give up her baby to ensure its survival. Marcus only hoped that we'd made as wise a decision in giving up our "baby" in Montgomery for the unknown undertaking awaiting us in Dallas. We gave up a great deal in Montgomery. Plus, the Christian buyers required us to do seller financing, so we struggled for several years to pay off all our creditors. We also surrendered the daily ministry program and the pulpit it provided for reaching so many people with God's Word.

When Marcus first told me about the Lord's plan for us in Dallas, I was willing to do it; but neither of us had any idea where we would get the financing that such a move would require, especially since we'd made no money on the Montgomery sale. It seemed impossible at first. We had the faith, but the bankers needed more than that.

We learned that there was a permit for a station in the Dallas area for sale, but it was priced at over a million dollars. We needed $10,000 just to bind the contract to purchase the permit—and we didn't have that either. To add to the pressure, we had only a week to come up with the $10,000 because the guy selling the permit said he had another potential buyer.

Again we surrendered this grand plan and all of the financial requirements to the Lord, figuring He was going to lead us to this station in Dallas in His own good time, through His own means. It seemed a little crazy then to enter into a contract for more than a million dollars when we didn't even have the $10,000 for the earnest money, and it still does today. But Marcus knew the Lord would guide us penny by penny. We prayed and the answer came. The Lord reminded Marcus that, as a college graduation present from his parents, he had been given five acres of rural land that was a part of his family's homestead outside Macon, Georgia. Marcus had never dreamed of selling the land because it was part of his family's heritage. There was even a road named Marcus Road that cut through it. But the Lord had His own road in mind.

We talked about selling the land to raise the earnest money, but it didn't seem possible to pull off a transaction quickly enough to meet the one-week deadline. It takes time to survey the land, list with a Realtor, and complete all the other steps involved in getting property on the market. Even if we could quickly find a buyer, he or she would have to get approval for a loan and set up a closing, which usually takes more than a month.

But when you surrender your finances to the Lord's plan, some amazing things can happen. Marcus learned that his parents' neighbor had expressed an interest in adding to her property. He called her and asked if she would be interested in buying his five acres for $10,000.

"I'll buy it," she said.

Amazingly, she wrote a check for the full amount, and the deal was done in just a few days.

Ten thousand dollars was a lot of money for us to have in 1986, but there was no talk of doing anything but putting it toward the purchase of the station permit in Dallas. This was a surrender not only of that money, but also of Marcus's portion of the family homestead. The $10,000 allowed us to secure the permit to buy the station in Dallas that became the foundation of the Daystar Television Network. If we hadn't been willing to surrender the family land and the money that came from it, we might never have built what we have today.

Obstacles

We had to sell our house in Montgomery before we could move to Dallas and start building a television station there. We needed the money from that sale to finance a home in Dallas. We had a nice house in a good neighborhood, and we felt sad about leaving it. Still, we gladly followed the Lord's direction and put up a For Sale sign. We found a buyer and prepared to close. But on the very day we were supposed to close, the Alabama Department of Revenue garnished the equity from the sale of our home.

Several weeks before this closing, a man and woman came knocking on our door. Marcus greeted them, only to be informed that they were agents from the Alabama Department of Revenue, the state's version of the federal Internal Revenue Service. The revenue agents later informed Marcus that they were putting a lien on our house for $22,000 because they claimed we owed that much in back taxes. Marcus said it was one of the most difficult moments of his life when he had to tell me about the state's allegations. He was afraid I'd feel he had failed us somehow. But I know my husband. I had faith that Marcus always took care of business in an honest and upright manner.

The investigation meant we couldn't receive the proceeds from the sale of our own house until we got the matter straightened out. It also meant that we had to prove our innocence—that we did not owe any back taxes. We had received no prior warning of this. A letter giving notice came in the mail a few days *after* the revenue agents showed up on our doorstep. We had to wonder if the Enemy wasn't trying to block us from following the Lord's plan in Dallas, especially when the revenue agents informed us that they planned to audit all of our finances for the past five years.

It was embarrassing, frustrating, and scary, but we knew we had nothing to hide. So once again, we surrendered to God's will—and a very good accountant. The accountant told us that the state's revenue agents weren't even following their own tax laws in their claims against us. Apparently, they arbitrarily had disallowed exemptions that were legally ours to claim under state and federal laws. The accountant was outraged. He felt that we had been singled out because we were on Christian television.

While the accountants and lawyers fought it out, we struggled with what to do. We sold our home, but we couldn't collect our equity until this mess was straightened out. We had to get to Dallas where God had called us. So we ended up renting a U-Haul because we didn't have the money to hire a moving company. We drove to Dallas, pulling the U-Haul trailer behind our Honda Accord with our two kids in the back seat. Once there, we rented a two-bedroom apartment in Euless, outside Dallas, as a temporary home. It was tough because we were basically starting all over again, and this time we would be farther away from our families in South Carolina and Georgia; but we committed ourselves to the surrender, trusting that the Lord would work it out for us.

In the meantime, we had no money coming in, which was a real challenge. We got through that difficult time by remembering God's promise to Marcus: we would be blessed for selling our Montgomery station to the Christian buyers for the debt that was owed on it versus selling it for more money to a secular businessman, who would have turned it into a secular TV station. We kept the faith even as we struggled in the first few years in the Dallas area.

God Provides

In a God-ordained turn of events, our Alabama accountant became so incensed with the state's disregard for its own laws and regulations that he called the state tax commissioner and informed him that he would do whatever it took to see justice in our case and would not be charging us further for his services. Furthermore, he went to state officials with the evidence and all of our documentation. In the end the state agreed we had done nothing wrong. Marcus had always prepared all of our taxes, and the state found that he'd done them honestly and correctly. We didn't owe them a dollar. As a result, the Alabama Department of Revenue sent us a check for 100 percent of the money they garnished, plus interest.

Once our tax troubles were cleared up, we were able to start looking for a home and focus on our new life in suburban Dallas. Again, we had a struggle to get our new station, KMPX-TV 29, on the air. Our biggest challenge was getting a broadcast tower; but finally, after three years, we began broadcasting in 1993, from a leased studio in the Dallas Communications Complex.

God had sent us into the broadcast world at a time of great change in the industry. We bought KMPX just as federal deregulation was making more channels available in the market. The increased number of stations on the market resulted in lower prices. Just as the Lord guided us into Christian broadcasting, it became far less expensive to get into the market. At the same time, ownership restrictions were eased and UHF stations were made more equal to other broadcast entities. Another factor worked in our favor—cable television companies were required to carry local stations, giving us access to their subscribers. Even though it took us years to see it, the Lord's plan was working.

In August of 1997, our Dallas area ministry moved into a new 32,000-square-foot office facility. Then, on New Year's Eve, we officially launched the Daystar Television Network with our first live broadcast featuring Bishop T. D. Jakes preaching from The Potter's House in Dallas. With our success in Dallas, we were able to purchase a UHF station in Macon—Marcus's hometown—and then a noncommercial station in Denver. Those three stations were the foundation for Daystar.

In the year 2000, the FCC allowed twenty-four-hour religious programming on noncommercial television stations that could not sell advertising. Such stations are not as expensive to purchase, which made it possible for us to keep growing our network in major markets, gaining access to more viewers for the Lord's work. By late 2001, Daystar had grown to include eighteen television stations. By the end of 2002, we were broadcasting nationally on Direct TV and the Dish Network.

In March of 2003, Daystar launched on the Hot Bird 6 satellite, broadcasting into seventy-four countries, and on the Thaicom 3 satellite, broadcasting into fifty-nine countries. That December, we moved our headquarters into a new 90,000-square-foot International Ministry Center with two state-of-the-art production studios. Our new facility was located on a major freeway near the Dallas/Fort Worth International Airport.

By 2004 our broadcast ministry had become a network with TV stations in thirty-six cities around the country. Our satellite broadcasts also beamed into Europe and Asia. It took nearly ten years of challenging times, but God's plan finally began to work for us in amazing and wondrous ways. That same year, after a long period of negotiation and some brilliant decisions that Marcus made with the Lord's guidance, we did a simultaneous transaction that proved to be the blessing that God had promised us back in Montgomery.

KMPX-TV 29 was a full-power UHF commercial station with a limited broadcast range, so it wasn't exactly the perfect fit to cover all of the Dallas/Fort Worth Metroplex. But the Lord showed Marcus how to leverage KMPX to buy what was a much better station for us. We sold KMPX for $37 million and then used just $19.5 million of those proceeds to purchase KDTN, a more powerful noncommercial VHF station that could broadcast to a half million more viewers. It even came with the perfect call letters, KDTN, for the Daystar Television Network. Plus we were able to bank the $17.5 million difference, which funded our efforts to reach even more people with God's Word.

One of the challenges of surrender is that you have to be patient and wait for God to work His plan on His schedule. Often, as mere mortals, we cannot understand His ways. We grow impatient and confused and even angry when we lack understanding. But many times Marcus and I have been blessed when we have trusted and waited.

In our efforts to reach more people with Christian programming, we had filed with the FCC in September of 1996 for a permit to build another television station in a high-growth area, Phoenix, Arizona. It took more than three years for that process to unfold. We finally got the permit in December of 1999. This noncommercial station, which had strong coverage in the market, came to us at a bargain. It cost us only a few thousand dollars to apply and less than $1 million to build the station. (Isn't it funny how our perspectives change?)

Within a few short years, we were approached by several groups about selling that station because of the explosive growth in Phoenix. We didn't want to leave the Phoenix market because we felt it needed a voice for Christian broadcasting, so we ended up doing a deal with NBC, which is owned by General Electric, one of the five largest companies in the world! NBC, which was eager to reach more Hispanic viewers, needed a bigger broadcast presence in the booming region. In June of 2006, NBC traded us three smaller television stations in the Phoenix area for our single, larger, noncommercial station. It worked out well for both sides since we each obtained the stations that were best suited to our needs. Financially, it was an even better deal. They gave us $50 million plus the three TV stations for a combined value of $76 million, which was a pretty nice trade for our station, in which we'd only invested about $1 million.

As Marcus says, there is no way that we were ever smart enough or talented enough to pull off that kind of deal on our own. It was God's hand. He rewarded us for our faith and our surrender in financial matters to His will.

Marcus and I believe that all of the ministry's money and all of our personal money belongs to God and that we have to be good stewards with what the Lord has given us. We had many lean years when we lived as traveling evangelists, totally dependent on the Lord to meet our needs. And we have had many fruitful years. We have learned, in either case, to surrender all of our financial matters to His will and to always be aboveboard in our dealings. We are open about our finances and have our books audited by an independent accounting firm yearly. We always stress that our mission is not to make money; it is to do good works, to minister to people as an extension of the church, and to spread the good news of the gospel.

Now that we have more money coming in, we consider it our responsibility to give more away or to spend it in ways that honor and glorify the Lord and add to His kingdom. Daystar has given more than $21 million over the last few years to help people across America and around the world, including victims of 9/11, the tsunami, and Hurricane Katrina. We encourage our viewers to tithe to their local churches, not to send tithes to us. If they want to make a freewill and faith offering to us, then we will use that money to try to reach more people with God's Word. We want donations to Daystar to come from the heart, not out of compulsion or need. We have already been given so much from God; we want people to give only if they wish to partner with us and join in reaching others for Christ.

The process of financial surrender never ends. It only grows greater with the more blessings you have. Financial surrender can't be for your own glory. It must be for His. Some people believe that as they prosper they don't need to lean on God anymore, but He always wants us to be dependent upon Him. He always wants us to look to Him as our source. Isaiah 1:19 tells us, "If you are willing and obedient, you shall eat the good of the land."

1

The Path of Surrender

Surrender simply means to give up control. For many people, the thought of giving up control is a scary one. Who doesn't like to be in control, make their own decisions, and choose what the future holds?

That all sounds good, but I'd like to ask you a question before you run off deciding what you want to do with your life: do you believe there is a God?

I want to challenge you with the thought that God is concerned about you and your life.

There are always those naysayers who will tell you, "God doesn't care about me, nor is He concerned about my life." But for a moment, stop trying to figure out God.

This is a moment you should stop to consider the word *surrender* and at the same time catch a glimpse of the One who desires to be an intimate part of your life. It leads you to the place where you'll find the peace that you've wanted.

You have nothing to lose but fear, disappointment, and a lack of purpose, so take a journey in exploring this question:

Are you ready to live with more peace, power, and purpose?

A Beginning

Start by looking at the word *surrender.* The word has many powerful connotations. For some, the idea evokes fear. For others, it's a sign of weakness. Many consider surrender a failure and associate it with shame.

Surrender to God doesn't mean you will have to do something you are afraid of doing. He puts the dreams and desires in your heart so that you know whatever comes is right. If being a missionary in a third-world country isn't a dream or desire of yours, God won't ask you to do that. He will find the best way to use you to advance the kingdom of God.

Surrendering to God is not an act of weakness. God uses your submission to bring great power into your life.

There is a wonderful historical and biblical account about a woman named Esther—an account that I think of when I picture what the power in surrender means. Esther gives us a perfect example of a surrendered life. As a young, orphaned Jewish girl in a society that wasn't keen on her heritage, she accepted the assignment to prepare herself as a possible candidate to be queen. The king was looking for a wife, and there would be many young ladies that would go before him. Although the chances looked pretty slim that Esther would be chosen, she followed God's Path of Surrender. She had no idea that her God-given positioning would eventually give her the opportunity to save her people. But when Esther did become queen, she not only stepped up to what God called her to do but also touched the heart of the king, and she gained influence in a time and season that was pivotal for the Jewish people. Esther would later agree with her mentor and only surviving family member, Mordecai, who knew she was born "for such a time as this."

Today Esther is remembered as a woman who obeyed God with her future and in the process became a woman of great power and influence, whose bravery is forever etched in the hearts of the Jewish people.

Her example speaks to all of us that surrendering to God does not mean failure. She reminds us that God's laws are diametrically opposed to our carnal flesh. For instance, God says to love your enemies. Man says to hate your enemies. God says to forgive. Man says to not forgive. God says to bless those that curse you. Man says to curse those who curse you (see Luke 6:27–35). There are spiritual laws that supersede what our carnal flesh wants to do. The Bible says a carnal mind cannot understand the things of the Spirit (see 1 Corinthians 2:14). So your flesh will tell you that surrendering to God is failing or giving up, when in reality you are gaining everything in life that holds true value or significance. The truth is that instead of failing, you will succeed, and in the process you will find peace that passes all understanding.

Surrendering to God means allowing Him to do what He wants to do with your life; it puts you smack-dab in the center of God's will. There is no finer or more fulfilling experience than to be doing what He wants us to do.

All of us have impaired vision—not the sort of impairment that requires glasses, contacts, or laser surgery; but a limitation due to our humanity. We can't see what God sees. Most of us can hardly look ahead a month or two. It is difficult for me to plan a few weeks out because of our family's hectic schedule. Yet the Lord's view is infinite. God knows each of us before we appear in our mother's womb (see Jeremiah 1:5). He created us, from our toes to our talents. That difference between our vision and God's vision is what Texans call a "whoppin' difference."

The Path of Surrender

When we agree to follow God's plan, the impact is eternal. Surrender takes us out of the earthly realm and beyond our own capacity to understand the vast implications and puts us on a path to eternity. Giving our gifts back to God frees Him to put them to their highest use with His infinite power and wisdom.

Step 1: Acknowledge Your Need for God

The first step in the Path of Surrender is to believe in God and to acknowledge that there is a void in you that only He can fill.

Think of yourself as a puzzle and God as the four important edge pieces. If God is not a part of your life, you feel an aching emptiness and a lack of direction, which can affect your relationships, your career, your emotions, your health. Some have never considered framing their lives with God's plan; others lost God's purpose by falling into ungodly living.

At the ripe old age of eighteen, I'd reached that critical first step in the Path of Surrender. I was a believer and I loved God, but I didn't know how desperately I needed Him. All my attention was on the young man I had met and would continue to date for two years.

This guy, a popular guy a bit older than I, first saw me at homecoming when I was a high school senior, and he called me for a date. I was performing in a church play that night and invited him to come along. To my surprise, he agreed. He got all dressed up and sat with my mom and dad. It must have been way out of his comfort zone, and I had to give him credit for doing it. After the production, however, when he asked me to get something to eat, I turned him down. He was nice looking, but I just didn't feel comfortable around him. I told him that the cast was going out and that I'd better go with them.

I didn't hear from him for three months. Then one day he called me again and asked if I would go out with him. I wasn't dating anyone at the time, and I'd felt a little guilty about how I'd treated him, so we went out and the courtship began. I grew comfortable with him. He was a perfect gentleman who went to church with me and called me every day. He was kind and considerate.

Six months later I thought I was in love with this young man. Some of my friends questioned the relationship. My parents, who liked him initially, began to doubt his sincerity. I told my doubting friends and parents that they had no proof he was a bad person, and I ignored my own growing sense of unease.

I had never partied or smoked or drank or done drugs. My social life had always been centered on family, friends, church, and youth group activities. My love for God was very strong. I knew it wasn't the same for my boyfriend, but I thought men had to be a certain way until they finally settled down. He didn't hide the fact that when he was away from me, he smoked, drank, and partied—and I knew he was pushing and pulling me in ways that conflicted with my value system. I consoled myself with the fact that he claimed to be a Christian, he went to church with me, and he treated me well. Plus, like so many young women, I thought I could fix the man in my life.

Finally, God decided that I needed a wake-up call. One night we went with another couple to a restaurant where they also had music and danc-ing. I loved to dance. When we sat down to dinner, the other girl's boyfriend asked me to keep his car keys in my purse because his date had left her purse in the car. We ate and then danced until it was time for me to get home. I had an earlier curfew, at 11:00 p.m., so my boyfriend took me in his car and dropped me off.

Just as I walked in the side door, the other girl's date called and said that I still had his car keys in my purse. It was a pretty long drive back to the restaurant, so I thought I'd just jump in my car and catch up to my boyfriend, give him the keys, and let him take them back to our friend. I drove toward my boyfriend's house, thinking that's where he had gone, but on the way I noticed his Camaro parked in front of a pool hall and bar. I pulled up next to it, and there he was standing next to his car with his arm around a girl.

You can imagine the look on his face when he saw me. He pushed her away and asked me what I was doing there. I threw our friend's car keys at him, but before I could drive away, he put his head in my window and started talking to me to keep me from leaving. I threatened to run him over, and he stepped back. My little Mustang had never been driven so fast in reverse.

The next day he called and of course had every excuse. He told me he really wasn't doing anything and confessed his undying love for me. My eyes had been opened, but my heart needed more convincing. The trust was gone, but he persisted, giving me all the typical excuses and professing his love for me. We argued, made up, and argued some more in a cycle that kept repeating itself in the weeks that followed.

I had been trying so hard to fix my relationship with this young man, but what I really needed to do was to fix my relationship with the Lord.

And that's when I took my first step on the Path of Surrender: I realized my boyfriend would never fill the emptiness inside of me—and, more importantly—that only God could.

Step 2: Offer a Prayer of Surrender

Once you realize how much you need the Lord, the next step is to ask for God's help and intervention. You can't surrender to His will until you invite the Lord to forgive your sins and to come into your heart and your life. This isn't a one-time deal. It needs to be repeated every time you face a challenge in any aspect of your life.

The first time I took this step in the process I was twenty, shortly after the night I saw my boyfriend for what he really was and not what I had wanted him to be. I wrote a letter to the Lord, pouring out my heart and telling Him that I needed help getting back on the proper path:

July 21, 1980
11:26 p.m.

I really don't have any idea why I'm writing this, except that I have so much in my heart that I need to say. I wonder over and over again what my life holds and where I'm going. I feel so confused about everything, especially my feelings. I wonder deep in my heart if I'll ever be able to love any man the way I loved him. Deep inside, I know it's better we're apart, but, oh, how my heart burns with pain. I thank the Lord for helping me this far. I pray He'll help me further.

Sometimes I pray the Lord just let me die and go to heaven to be with Him. I'm so tired of this old world full of sin. But, oh, how selfish I sound. There are so many other people that need to hear about Jesus.

Dear Lord, take my life, use me in whatever way, and I pray You show me the path to follow. I know I don't always understand, but Lord I know You loved me enough to die for me. Oh God, I put my faith in You, and I know with Your hand, my life can be in Your perfect will. I pray I can be close to You always—I love You, Lord Jesus. Thank You for hearing my prayer.

This letter was my spontaneous Prayer of Surrender; I put that letter under my mattress.

God's call to you may be different than His to me, but if you are listening, you will hear your spiritual alarm going off. When you do, offer your own Prayer of Surrender. It is the proper and only response. Your prayer can be spoken, sung, or delivered in whatever form works best for you—as long as it is heartfelt. It can be as simple as saying: "I ask Your forgiveness of my sins. I believe You sent Your Son to die on the cross for my sins. I commit to doing Your will by surrendering my life to You."

I encourage you to write your own Prayer of Surrender in the form of a letter. At the end of this book, there is a page for you to write your personal letter to the Lord, if you choose. Of course, there is not one correct way to do this, but a guideline I suggest is to follow the ABCs:

Ask for God's forgiveness for your sins.

Believe that His Son died on the cross for your sins.

Commit to surrendering your life to His will.

A lot of people know of God, just as most people know who our president is. Imagine, though, if you were to go up the White House steps, knock on the door, and say, "I'm here to see the president." Chances are the president doesn't know you personally, and you'll be escorted off the grounds. Likewise, many people know who God is, but they don't know Him personally. They haven't invited Him into their hearts and into their lives.

To know God in your heart and soul, you have to ask for His forgiveness, believing that He sent His Son to die on the cross for your sins. And then you have to commit to following the path that He sends you upon.

It is one thing to know the Lord's name; it is an entirely different matter to put your life in His hands. In Matthew 7:21–23, Jesus tells us: "Not everyone who says to me, 'Lord, Lord,' will enter the kingdom of heaven, but only he who does the will of my Father who is in heaven. Many will say to me on that day, 'Lord, Lord, did we not prophesy in your name, and in your name drive out demons and perform many miracles?' Then I will tell them plainly, 'I never knew you. Away from me, you evildoers!' " (NIV).

Many throw around the name of God in a show of piety, but He knows the difference between a name-dropper and a believer. When we get to heaven we will probably all be surprised to find that some who appeared pious were not godly in their hearts, while others who did not sit in the first pews in church are granted entrance to His kingdom because of where they sat with the Lord.

Step 3: Use Your Gifts

After you offer your Prayer of Surrender, the next step is to wait, watch, and pray for God's plan to reveal itself to you. God most likely won't send a lightning bolt or open the heavens to speak from above. God is more subtle than that. The way He often works is by giving gifts and talents. Turn on the GPS or your "Gifts Positioning System." Follow your gifts down the road and see what blessings come.

God endowed you with unique gifts and dreams and desires, and He is not going to let them go to waste, especially once you have surrendered your will to His. For instance, He would not bless you with a brilliant mind for mathematics, if He didn't have a plan for using that gift. Nor would God bless you with a gorgeous singing voice if He didn't want to use it to bless and encourage others. Instead, He will put you in a position to use your talents to His highest glory and to live the dreams He's given you.

When you find yourself on a path that fulfills you, brings you joy, and maximizes your abilities to put God's gifts to work, you can be confident that the Lord is lighting the way.

The Bible says, "A gift opens the way for the giver and ushers him into the presence of the great" (Proverbs 18:16, NIV). Will those blessings come in the form of money in the bank and material things piling up in the garage? Not necessarily. God may bless you with things that money can't buy, such as good health, loving children, service to others, a blessed marriage.

In 3 John 2–4, Jesus says: "Beloved, I pray that you may prosper in all things and be in health, just as your soul prospers. For I rejoiced greatly when brethren came and testified of the truth that is in you, just as you walk in the truth. I have no greater joy than to hear that my children walk in truth."

You are born with your gifts, but sometimes they lie dormant or undiscovered until you surrender to God's plan for you. Once you have surrendered, you will find your talents blossoming and doors opening to undreamed of opportunities. God may present new dreams to you as well, taking you places that were beyond your ability to see. In Psalm 37:4–6, we are told: "Delight yourself in the LORD and he will give you the desires of your heart. Commit your way to the LORD; trust in him and he will do this: He will make your righteousness shine like the dawn, the justice of your cause like the noonday sun" (NIV). Best of all, you will experience peace and joy in these new ventures because you know God's plan is good.

I surrendered in my letter to the Lord, but I still did not know the desires of my own heart. I felt that my relationship with my boyfriend wasn't going anywhere unless he changed dramatically, but I didn't take any action yet. I watched, waited, and prayed. During this transition time, I should have been at wit's end, but knowing I was in God's hands, I felt an amazing sense of peace.

I was out of school and working in the office of an engineering firm. I started at the bottom of the company as a "runner" for the engineers and eventually was promoted to a data technician position in the purchasing department, working for several of the buyers. Now I realize how God used that season in my life to hone my secretarial skills—skills that I would use again and again in my present-day world with e-mail, letters, and now writing a book.

You may feel like you're spinning your wheels, but let me assure you that God will use every one of your life experiences in preparation for what He has for you. Within just a few months of writing my own personal surrender letter to the Lord at age twenty, He put me on a path that I had never imagined for myself. In fact, while rereading my letter, I had to chuckle. There I was at twenty years of age wanting to go be with the Lord. Ah, the drama. I can say that, laughing, now. But I couldn't have said or heard that then, because then I felt like my life was out of order and the choices I'd made weren't working. The inner struggle was real, and I knew that God was trying to show me something. The problem was I couldn't see what my future held, and what I saw and what God saw were vastly different things. It would have been easy to surrender if I could have looked through the telescope of time and viewed the awesome plan God had for me. But I couldn't see the future, and it was time for God to see if he could trust me to trust Him…and there, my friend, is the key.

Are you ready to trust God? Can He trust you to put Him first, even when you don't know what the future holds?

When I wrote that letter of surrender, my life changed. Not overnight, but over time—and forever. The words "Take my life… I put my faith in You, and I know with Your hand, my life can be in Your perfect will" were some of the most powerful I ever uttered. That was my moment of total surrender to God. I was saying in essence, "Take my life and do what You want to do with it"—and guess what?

God did. He took me at my word, and I had no idea what the future held—but it would be beyond my wildest dreams.

Just a few months after I wrote that letter, on a Sunday morning in October 1980, our church had a revival. I was sitting way in the back of the church, but the young evangelist was so dynamic that he had my full attention. At this point I was still hoping I could somehow "fix" my boyfriend, and I thought this evangelist might be able to reach him. I decided to ask him to go to the revival with me that evening. I prepared a little speech about how I wanted him to go to help our relationship. I called him on the telephone to ask him, but before I could get into my pitch about how good this evangelist would be for him, he said he wasn't interested.

"I have plans. I'm going to watch a ballgame with the guys," he said.

I persisted. He resisted.

"Joni, please, I go to church things with you all the time, but I have plans tonight so just drop it. I'm not going."

It certainly wasn't our worst disagreement, but he made it clear to me in that conversation that he wasn't at all committed to putting God at the center of his life. I knew we were at the end of our relationship. It was time to break up. I had no idea what I would do with myself once our relationship was over, but I felt determined to put an end to it.

He was already at his friend's house, so I grabbed my car keys and headed over there. My mom told me later that she had never seen such determination on my face as when I walked through the kitchen and out the side door. When I showed up, he was shocked to see me, of course. I'd never been confrontational or big on drama in our relationship—and I'm sure he never expected me to be the one to call it quits.

"I can't believe you are getting so mad over this," he said, after getting in my car to talk.

I explained that it wasn't just his refusal to go to church with me that night. "Our relationship isn't going to work," I told him. "We are so different. I want to follow God's path. You don't. If we ever got married and raised kids, we would have two different sets of values. There is no way it would work out."

That was it for him. "If you want to break up that's fine," he said angrily. "You can take your God and shove Him." He got out of the car, slammed the door, and walked away.

It was a dramatic moment, and really, a crossroads. As I drove home, crying, I bawled, "It's just You and me, Lord."

God must have been tickled at that. I was only twenty years old, so I'm sure He understood that my life was hardly as bad as it seemed. Still, I cried and prayed all night, missing the revival meeting. I worked late the next two nights, trying to keep myself occupied, but on Wednesday my mother called and asked me to go to the service that night at the church. The same young evangelist was speaking, and the revival was to continue the rest of the week.

"This has just been the most amazing revival," she said. "It'll do you good."

I was glad to go and pray and have my spirits lifted. I sat about halfway back this time, on the right side; and though there was a good crowd in the church, I had a little better view of the preacher standing up onstage. He looked even younger and more handsome than I remembered, and his message spoke even more powerfully to me than last time.

After the sermon that night, hot dogs were served in the church fellowship hall. I was helping out in the kitchen, surprised at how happy I felt so soon after the breakup. I knew I was on the right path. "Joni," said one of the girls as she came into the kitchen, "I'm supposed to ask you if you would like to come out and talk to the evangelist. He said he'd like to meet you."

I smiled. The poor guy was probably tired of talking to all the old folks who were hovering around him all the time. Because the services were going so well, the revival was extended for another week, so this would give him an opportunity to connect with some of the younger people. I finished what I was doing, and then went out to the fellowship hall to meet him. We exchanged handshakes and greetings, but he was surrounded by people, so we didn't talk much.

In recounting this story, it's funny to think about that very first Sunday morning service we attended where this young evangelist had been speaking. I had ridden to church with my parents, and after the service we started to leave. I was sitting in the back of the car when the evangelist saw my parents and waved to them across the parking lot.

"He's so friendly," my mother said. "Isn't he handsome?" She turned around and gave me one of those motherly looks and said, "Would you ever consider dating someone like him?"

"Mother!" I couldn't believe it. "I don't even know if he's single; besides, he's too short!"

But my mother's intuition proved to be right. After the Wednesday night service, the young man called my house. My four-year-old brother answered the phone and told him that I was working late, so I didn't get the message. After the revival service the next night, the evangelist motioned me over to the piano. As I stood there, he reached his hand across the piano and said, "Would you like to go get something to eat?"

It was a little uncomfortable for me to be singled out with all the other people around, and I really didn't know what to think about being asked to dinner by a preacher, even if he was young and good looking, but I agreed.

When we met up after the service and stood face to face—me in my four-inch-heel black boots—I realized we had a problem. As charming and handsome as this man was, he was not tall. At all. At that age, I had a big hang-up about height. I'm five feet eight inches tall, which isn't especially tall, but I'd always dated guys who were more than six feet. My father and grandfather were about six foot four. But it was too late to back out now.

He went out to get his car and then picked me up at the church door. As we drove to Mr. Gaddy's, a pizza place, I was fixated on the fact that he was short. But as we walked in and stood in line to order our pizza, he didn't seem so short after all—he was actually the same height as I was. I looked down and saw that he'd made a quick change into a pair of high-heeled cowboy boots!

Marcus likes to say that's when I fell head over "heels" for him! And it's certainly true that he had all my attention. But to be entirely truthful, even though Marcus elevated his game by putting on his boots, I didn't realize that God had put me on a new path. Marcus intimidated me. He was definitely much more a man of God than I'd ever dated. He had a theology degree, even though he was only three years older than I. His commitment and his knowledge of the Bible were far greater than mine. Going from my previous boyfriend to him was like spiritual whiplash.

On that first night he did his best to put me at ease. We didn't talk about Jesus nearly as much as we laughed and talked about the usual getting-to-know-you stuff. He had a great sense of humor, which was refreshing and helped me relax. He even joked about the fact that other girls had tried to impress him on first dates by showing him how many Bible verses they could quote. I liked that he seemed to have a lot of ambition and drive. He'd graduated from high school at sixteen and got his theological degree from Lee University three years later, graduating magna cum laude. He was definitely a guy with big plans and a lot of energy and charisma.

After that first date, Marcus asked me out every night after the revival. I'd told him about my recent breakup, and Marcus made no bones about the fact that he wanted to make certain I didn't stray back—and seemed determined to keep me occupied.

Dating someone with the same value system who was willing to talk openly about his love of God was a whole new thing for me. And it was such a relief to no longer feel pressured with the carnal things. Even with all this, there was nothing "holier than thou" about Marcus. He talked a lot about his decision to enter the ministry and how he'd been conflicted. He'd wanted to be a doctor or a lawyer in his younger days. He'd even "argued" with God about it, but once he had surrendered to God's will, there was no doubt what God's plan was for Marcus.

My surrender to the Lord had led to our paths crossing, but it took me longer to surrender to Marcus.

Step 4: Be Prepared to Surrender Again and Again

When you have surrendered once, you will find that the next step is to surrender again. And again. And again. Along the Path of Surrender you will experience great joy as well as sweet salvation, but don't be fooled into thinking one surrender will cover all the challenges that lie along the road to heaven. The Christian life is one of continual surrender. You will need to go through this process at every crossroads, every bump in the road, every challenge in your life.

At the first moment of surrender, the Lord doesn't usually reveal the entire path to us—which is a good thing. We often have to grow into the roles that He designs for us. It might be too scary to get the whole picture right out of the box. We have to be patient and let God work His way. The Lord had a lot in store for me, and He is still revealing things to me more than twenty-five years after my initial surrender.

With my first surrender, I put my trust in God and told myself that He would make a way for me. After I met Marcus, my head was spinning. With my old boyfriend, it was as if I had been standing on a table trying to pull him up to my spiritual level. The weight of his reluctance eventually made me weary until, in the end, he was pulling me down and away from my faith. Now Marcus was on the table, pulling me back up. I was willing, so I wasn't pulling Marcus down, but it wasn't easy either. Now we were basically on the same level with the same goals, the same love for God, and a deep desire to be used by God—but to remain in Marcus's life, I had to be willing to surrender my entire life to the Lord. Marcus felt he had to be certain about me because the relationships of ministers are so scrutinized. He didn't want to make a mistake and neither did I.

Also, I had to be willing to let go of my old boyfriend, but that wasn't very difficult to do, because once you've experienced someone with your same passion, you don't want to go backward and settle for less. After the revival was over, Marcus moved on to the next revival in another state, and we began a long-distance relationship. We were drawn to each other, and we both felt that we were falling in love, but it was difficult for us to forge strong bonds when we were apart so much of the time. We dated from that October through the month of May, and I began to get frustrated. We talked on the telephone nearly every day, and we saw each other whenever Marcus could get back into town, but he didn't seem capable of committing to our relationship for the long term.

Later, Marcus would tell me that he was genuinely scared of a commitment, but at this point we both loved each other and there was nowhere to go except to the next step of an engagement. He was fearful of that next step, and I was unwilling to sit around and wait, so we agreed to break up—which was another surrender. I had no idea what the future held for me, and at times I questioned God, wondering where my life was going.

Marcus and I still talked regularly and saw each other occasionally, but I dated some other guys that summer. Feeling unsettled was difficult for me, but God was teaching me how to look to Him. The hard thing about surrender is that you don't always know what is going on. You have to trust God when everything isn't going perfect. Later, my mother-in-law told me that she knew Marcus and I would eventually get married. She had prayed and was assured that we would one day be together. I kidded her later, "Why didn't you tell me that?"

After we broke up, Marcus had a change of heart. He worried that his failure to commit had been a mistake and that he might lose me. He signed up for a cheap long-distance phone service so he could call me all the time for a flat fee. However, the reception was staticky and he'd get cut off after fifteen minutes with no notice, which drove us both a little crazy. Then he went overboard! He started calling my mother and my best friend and my siblings—anyone who could keep him updated on whether any other guy had caught my eye.

Three months later, Marcus couldn't take it anymore. He'd lost about fifteen pounds, and he didn't really have fifteen pounds to spare. We got together one weekend, and he poured out his heart, saying that he missed me too much—and I felt the same way. On the following Valentine's Day we went to a Chinese restaurant. By some miracle—or crafty planning by a certain evangelist—my fortune cookie contained a message that read: "Joni Lynn, will you marry me?" Marcus sealed the deal with a box of candy featuring a diamond as the centerpiece!

I was ready. I felt my love and I felt Marcus's love, but I trusted and depended on the Lord.

I had to surrender to the Lord many more times, of course. Even when it was obvious to both Marcus and me that we were made for each other, we had challenges. That's life. That is why it is so critical to understand the Path of Surrender. In your surrender, you will feel His presence and your faith will see you through.

2

A Heritage of Surrender

E. C. Trammell never knew his mother. She died while giving birth to him on their farm in South Carolina. E. C.'s father committed suicide six years later. The little boy struggled with never knowing his mother and never having his dad to grow up with.

When he was nine years old, hoeing in a farm field, breaking up clods of dirt on a sweltering July afternoon, E. C. suddenly reeled with an overwhelming feeling that no one loved him or even cared whether he lived or died. Paralyzing sorrow swept over him, and he felt as though he were going to pass out and fall into the dirt.

But then something changed. "I began to hear the most beautiful music, like angels singing," he recalls. "And then there was a voice that came not from above or around me but from inside my head. It wasn't something I heard so much as I felt. I guess if God had spoken aloud to me it would not have been any clearer. I knew in that instant, without any doubt, that God loved me."

Altered Destiny

My paternal grandfather, E. C. Trammell, was in his seventies when he told me his story—a story that happened long before I was born, but ultimately affected my own life in a profound way. That incident in the field was my grandfather's first step in the lifelong process of surrendering to God.

When he told me that story, I was a grown woman, so it struck me that we'd had similar awakenings to God's presence as children. I have heard many similar stories over the years from grown-up Christians who have never forgotten the instant when our heavenly Father made Himself known to them. Many continue, as my grandfather did, to tell me about the next step in the surrender process.

Grandpa Trammell was nineteen and working in a mill, surrounded by his co-workers. It was hard and tedious labor, and he was having difficulty focusing. His mind was restless. He felt disoriented. He went to a water fountain to get a drink and clear his head. A dark wave of despondency swept over him and, without even thinking about it, he cried out to the Lord from the crowded mill floor.

"God, if You are there, I want You in my life," he said. "I have done bad things. I have made many mistakes. Please, I am asking You to forgive me. Come into my life."

The room in that mill seemed to suddenly radiate light, but Grandfather shrugged and smiled a little as he told me about it. "Maybe it was just the sun coming through a window."

Sensing that God was listening, my grandfather asked not just for forgiveness but also guidance. He particularly asked the Lord to help him stop cursing. He had a bad mouth. "How can I be a witness for You when I talk like this?" he asked. "From that moment to this," Grandfather told me, "I never uttered another curse word."

Before any one of us can surrender to Jesus, we must acknowledge Him and welcome His presence in all that we do. That is an important aspect of our Christian faith. Many people understand God's grace and mercy and love, but they don't want to think about His judgment of their actions and their accountability to Him. We must strike a balance. And the way to reach that balance and to live in harmony with our Christian faith is to surrender every aspect of our lives to Him—not once in our lives, not just in "special" moments, but every minute of every day.

What makes my grandfather's surrender especially powerful and encouraging is that he had never been to church. He had no knowledge of God. So no matter where you are in your journey of faith, there is hope for you too. You don't have to fit into some kind of system. Wherever you are, God can still hear you if you only will cry out. Matthew 11:28–30 promises, "Come to Me all you who labor and are heavy laden, and I will give you rest. Take My yoke upon you and learn from Me, for I am gentle and lowly in heart, and you will find rest for your souls. For My yoke is easy and My burden is light."

My grandfather, who had never read the Bible and who had no training in prayer, was transformed by God's forgiveness and love as he stood, not in a great cathedral or even a small church, but in a mill.

As a nine-year-old boy in the field, he acknowledged God's presence in his life. But it took him ten more years to first surrender to the Lord. His surrender changed his life forever—and it changed the destiny of our whole family, and perhaps hundreds, thousands, and even millions of others.

Altering the Destiny of Others

Living in a constant state of surrender to God is important because what we do in our day-to-day lives sends ripples through the lives of those around us and those who will follow us.

Grandpa Trammell became a godly man. He raised my father—and six daughters—to be godly people too. As a result, I grew up with Christian grandparents and parents. The church Grandfather joined became the church where my father worshiped and the church where I worshiped. It was that very same church where I met my husband, Marcus.

The Bible says that God will bless your children and your children's children (see Psalm 112:2). I have reaped the benefits of the choices my grandfather made—and so have my children. All of my grandfather's grandchildren have benefited and so have all of their children—more than twenty of them.

It's like the modern retelling of "the loaves and the fishes" parable, in which God's blessings are multiplied many times over. I think of our family as a beautiful tapestry woven together by God's love and His presence in our lives. The Creator connects us all. Starting with my grandfather, our Christian family has come together through marriages and children into this amazing, living thing of beauty that will endure forever as God's own heirloom.

A Christian upbringing certainly makes things more conducive to living righteous lives, but this is a world fraught with temptation and sin. We all are capable of stumbling and falling from grace. My father veered off course as a teenager, which is a time when so many men and women experience crises of faith. He married my mother when he was twenty-one. She was fifteen. They weren't serving the Lord when I was born, but they found their way back to the church. As the Bible says in Proverbs 22:6: "Train up a child in the way he should go, and when he is old he will not depart from it."

Grandpa Trammell probably had that passage in mind when he told me, "Don't ever let go of the Lord's hand." Then he added these reassuring words: "If you want to get away from God, you will have to be the one to let go because He will never let go of you." Those words have always stayed with me.

When we fail to surrender our own lives to our Creator, that too can have a profound negative effect on others who are destined to be connected to our purpose. When we lack faith or falter in our faith, it not only affects our lives, it impacts all who fall within our spheres of influence.

I was talking about the power of surrender recently with some of our singers, and one of them offered the thought that if Marcus and I had not surrendered to God's plans for us, Daystar might never have come into existence. I'm sure that God would have built this Christian network through someone else if we were not available. He certainly is not limited to using us as His tools. Still, it is awe-inspiring to consider that my grandfather's act of faith and his surrender to God's plan for him led, two generations later, to a Christian broadcasting network that reaches countless people around the world.

Surrendering to your Creator will have a direct impact upon eternity and all who live in it.

Eddie Coronado

Of all the stories of surrender within the Daystar family, none are more inspiring or compelling than that of singer Eddie Coronado, whose heritage is so different from my own.

I've had the opportunity to take the singers and our band to several women's prisons to minister, and it's always interesting for me to watch the ladies as Eddie begins to share his story of God's grace and love in his life. One particular service was at the Hobby Unit, a women's prison near

Waco, Texas. As we opened the service with ministering, singing, and sharing, a Hispanic woman in the front row was one of the few who didn't respond with enthusiasm. She sat with arms crossed and a scowl on her face. She wouldn't even make eye contact with those of us on stage. Hundreds of other women in the audience were lifting their hands to the Lord, but this one woman was not moved—until Eddie stepped forward and started sharing his story of surrender. He immediately captured her attention, and when he interrupted his narrative to sing a Spanish inspirational song, I thought this woman would melt in her seat. Tears ran down her face and the faces of many of the others present, including me.

Tears of a Clown

Eddie was born in East Los Angeles in 1969, into a family that was mired in drugs, alcohol, and criminal activity. His father was not there for his birth because he was being held in jail awaiting trial on charges of murder. "It was a broken setting," Eddie explains, "but it hadn't started that way. I researched my family and found that my grandfather had worked for the customs agency in Mexico and that my older uncles had gone to school for accounting and other middle-class jobs."

His family's decline began with an act of honesty. Eddie's grandfather, who had a history of helping poor people but took his customs job seriously, was working at a border gate one day when he turned away a truck that didn't have the proper paperwork. The truck was loaded with fine furniture, but the taxes on it had not been paid. It turned out that the furniture belonged to his grandfather's supervisor, a commander in the customs unit. When the commander learned that his delivery had been turned back, he confronted Eddie's grandfather and physically attacked him. Eddie's grandfather defended himself and, sadly, killed his commander in the process.

"Because his commander came from a wealthy, influential family in the city, my grandfather, whom I never knew, got thirty years in prison. My grandmother lost everything. My older uncles left out of embarrassment and shame, and only my father and his two younger siblings remained."

Eddie's father was just eight years old when this happened. He grew up without a father or older brothers in the house. Looking for a substitute, he joined a street gang in Juarez and served as a drug courier for them. Eddie's father grew up in the streets, drinking, doing drugs, and serving the gang leaders. He was in and out of detention facilities. He often slept under cars or bridges rather than going home. Eventually his mother took the younger siblings and moved away, leaving Eddie's father behind and on his own to be raised by the streets of Juarez, Mexico.

Years passed before he met and married Eddie's mother and they moved to East L.A., where two of Eddie's uncles had moved and begun their illegal drug activities. Eddie was born in East L.A., and his father was released from prison shortly after Eddie's birth because no witnesses would testify against him.

These were horrible years. Eddie's mother and older siblings lived a nightmare. Eddie's brother, the oldest, was terrorized by their father, who constantly found any reason to hit him and hold him in fear.

"I recall my brother telling me of a time when he developed a boil on the back of his leg," Eddie says, "and my father got upset because he felt my brother needed to toughen up. So my father began squeezing the boil, and if my brother cried out, which he did, my father would hit him. He would repeat the process until my brother wouldn't cry."

This was when Eddie's brother was seven years old.

Eddie's mother also shared with him that she had a miscarriage at the hands of his father—an event triggering a deep depression and enslaving her to the mercy of someone who was constantly under the influence of hard drugs, alcohol, and rage. Although she feared for her life if she were to try and leave, when she conceived Eddie, she wanted to do whatever it took to keep him safe, so she looked for an opportunity to leave.

She found it when Eddie was five and his father was shot. While Eddie's father was still in the hospital, his mother saw an escape from the years of mental and physical abuse that she and her family had endured. She moved her children back to Juarez where she had family.

It was during this period that one of Eddie's uncles took him under his wing. This uncle loved to sing, and when he practiced, Eddie would sit by the bedroom door and listen. Eddie's sadness and greatest battle was triggered by his uncle, the same man who sparked Eddie's interest in singing. After winning the boy's confidence and trust, he stripped Eddie of his innocence, violating him and threatening him if he told anyone. "He created an atmosphere of fear and guilt so that I couldn't even tell my mother," Eddie recalls. "I felt so alone. There was no one for me to talk to. No one I could trust."

Sexual assaults and the sexual predator's evil corrupted Eddie at a young age. He got into trouble in school, fighting, and getting expelled. He was living in a lethal environment. Eddie's oldest brother was nearly killed in a gang fight—something he calls a normal occurrence.

"My favorite song to sing was 'Tears of a Clown' by Smokey Robinson," Eddie recalls. "Incredibly, the song came to make sense to me as a kid, particularly the line, 'if there's a smile on my face, it's only there trying to fool the public.' But even then, whenever I would cry and sing that song, I had the feeling that Someone was with me. Sometimes the presence was so strong I'd look around to see who was there."

One night Eddie was awakened by someone calling his name through a bedroom window. It was his father. But his mother heard him too, and she grabbed Eddie so that his father could not lure him away. "You're not going to take him away from me," she yelled.

"I remember feeling torn," says Eddie. "I wanted to talk to him so desperately and tell him everything that was happening. I wanted him to be with us. I didn't care if he was drunk or not."

Tears of Freedom

It was around the same time when things seemed to be at their worst that God stepped in. An evangelistic team came into Eddie's neighborhood and began witnessing to the young gang members. One of them was Eddie's oldest brother who had risen to be one of the leaders of the neighborhood gang. "One day my brother came home excited and happy. I'd never seen him like that before," Eddie remembers. Eddie's mother came in and told him to get dressed because they were going to church. "We walked out the front door and there in front of me was a white van with the words The Upper Room."

Eddie's life was about to change. He was eight years old.

"When we were driving up to this church I heard music, and it sounded like a party in the neighborhood, so I looked around thinking there was a festival," Eddie recalls. "We pulled up and there was the church, an old white brick industrial building. The sign read: The Upper Room. When we walked in the doors, I felt this rush of wind and as it hit me, I felt that presence again, the same one I'd felt when I sang by myself."

It was the first Christian service Eddie attended, and the music entranced him. But when the pastor talked about Christ's love for all people, Eddie cried. He wept through the entire service. "He was talking about Christ coming down from heaven and dying for our sins, and I felt dirty and ashamed. But then the pastor said in Spanish, 'God wants you just the way you are,' and it seemed so real. Even to this day when I think of those words, I break down." Eddie pauses, then continues. "You see, being raised Catholic we were taught to go to the priest for confession, but the fear my uncle had imbedded in my mind isolated me from anyone. On that night I learned that I could go to Christ myself, and He would be there for me no matter what."

Eddie and his mother and siblings answered the altar call, and they accepted the Lord that night. "I knelt down weeping at the altar, telling God that I didn't want to leave that place. It felt like home. I finally belonged somewhere. God spoke to my heart and told me that I only had to call to Him and He would be there for me."

Tears of Trial

Still, life did not get any easier for Eddie. When his father found out that his mother was taking the kids to the church, he fought it, threatening her life and beating her every chance he got. They were constantly moving and trying to hide.

"My mother was so strong," Eddie recalls. "She never thought of divorcing my father. She spent her time praying for him. I would hear her in the middle of the night, weeping and praying for him, turning him over to God's hands, saying, 'Have Your way—any way You can.'"

Any way was not how anyone imagined.

Soon after her prayer, Eddie's father was stricken with cirrhosis of the liver.

"Slowly I saw God work on our family," Eddie says. "My father wasn't living with us but was hospitalized. The doctors said he could not go another day because his liver was a mess. Then he showed up one day and he was different. He was sober and looked brighter. He told us later that he had seen an evangelical program on TV announcing a crusade in El Paso. He got up from the hospital bed and went to that crusade. While in the service the evangelist called out and said somebody there was dying of liver damage and that God was about to heal him. My father felt a warmth rush over him and fell under the power of God. That was more than thirty years ago, and my father is still alive. And my parents are together now."

Eddie's father surrendered to God—truly a miracle that started a long healing process for the family. But Eddie was not free and clear because of his father's return to God.

"It has been a slow and steady process for me," he explains. "I have gone through battles. As a teenager, I had a lot of unresolved anger and hatred. The things that happened at the hands of my uncle caused a lot of confusion for me. For a time I was very violent. I battled with pornography, lust, and confusion. I never got counseling, but I never let go of God's hand, and He never let go of mine."

At moments, Eddie "just wanted to disappear off the face of the earth." But God would tell him to "just hang on." He would find himself in church, reading the Bible while fending off his demons. "The Enemy would come at me hard," he remembers. "I could have taken the easy way out many times. Yet in my heart, I would hear God's voice telling me to hold on. I learned that a surrendered life doesn't have to be a perfect life. You just have to be willing to trust Him even when what you face is horrible. To God, that is part of the process."

Music was always the bridge that connected Eddie to the Lord. "Whenever I would sing, it would put me in a different place," he says. Eddie sang in church music programs and children's choirs, and his beautiful voice won him many admirers.

Tears of Healing

Years later Eddie's family moved to Sebring, Florida, where Eddie met and married his wife, Valarie, and soon after they had their son Malachi Israel. For a long time, singing was the only escape he had from a hardscrabble life. "For several years we were just existing. I worked in a lumberyard and as a customer service rep for an insurance company and at a pizza place and as a house painter. There was really no focus in our lives, except being together, but even that was difficult because I still had so many unresolved issues from my childhood. But God had a plan."

Adulthood brought more pain and anguish for Eddie. His oldest brother knew the Lord but had serious battles with drug addiction. The worst of these was heroin. Eddie's brother tried to kill himself several times. "I woke up and heard someone crying softly," Eddie says. "I got up and walked out of my bedroom and saw the silhouette of my brother in the living room. I turned on the light and saw one of the most horrific sights in my life. My brother had completely gashed his forearms open and was bleeding profusely in front of me."

Eddie learned that along with the physical and mental abuse his brother suffered with their father, he too had been molested—by another uncle in the family. Many dark and painful years lay ahead for Eddie and his family as they fought to save his brother's life and to help him defeat his demons of addiction and pain. His brother spent years addicted to heroin and other drugs before he surrendered to the Lord, and he is now working in a youth ministry in New York City.

Eddie's revelations about his own experiences gave his brother the courage to talk openly about what had happened to him. "Once I let people know about it, God started doing incredible things," Eddie says.

As he started talking about the abuse, Eddie learned that there had been a history of sexual predation among the family, and those who had preyed upon them had themselves been victims as children. As Eddie reached the age of thirty, most of his close family members had accepted Jesus Christ, including his siblings, uncles, parents, and even his ninety-year-old maternal grandmother. His Christian support network was getting stronger and stronger, helping to stabilize his life and giving Eddie the power to deal with the abuse he had endured as a vulnerable child. "I wish I could say that my healing came immediately, but I can't. What I can say is that even now, looking back, I wouldn't change anything in my life because the circumstances of my life and the pain I've endured are helping others be set free."

At the age of thirty, Eddie, with his wife and son, moved to Dallas, Texas, where he attended and graduated from Christ For The Nations Bible Institute. While there he was recruited to be a member of Living Praise, a select group of singers that traveled around the country. Eddie was on a trip to California with them when the Lord gave him a remarkable opportunity. "Our bus broke down at the Dream Center inner-city mission in Los Angeles, and I called my mom to let her know where I was. She freaked out and said that my grandfather lived just three miles away. So I called him and he picked me up," Eddie recalls.

Upon arriving at his grandfather's house, Eddie was stunned to learn that the uncle responsible for molesting him was living with his grandfather. "I thought, *I'm going to see him.* As I was getting my suitcase out of the car, my grandfather, who did not know what my uncle had done to me, said, 'There's your uncle.'"

Eddie looked up, expecting to see the towering menace that he remembered from his childhood. Instead, "he was this little man with a shaved head. He walked up to us and started talking, but he didn't make any sense," says Eddie, shaking his head. His uncle had become schizophrenic.

Eddie's uncle did not recognize him, and Eddie saw firsthand that the predator of his childhood had become a weak and fragile shell of his former self—and compassion filled Eddie's heart. That first encounter was brief, but it shook Eddie. He went to his grandfather's guest room and began praying. Eddie remembers, "I told God that if what my uncle was going through was the result of what he'd done to me, I didn't wish it upon him."

Eddie visited his grandfather for two more days. He also spent time with his uncle, his addled former abuser, who came to realize that Eddie was the child he had preyed upon. "On the last day we were sitting on my grandfather's porch talking, and I could tell that he was trying to say something, but because of his schizophrenia he wasn't making sense to me. His eyes filled with tears, and then I knew he was trying to tell me he was sorry. I put my arm around him and I prayed with him. I told him that he didn't have to carry the guilt of what had happened anymore."

In a testimony to his Christian faith, Eddie showed amazing strength. He surrendered his pain and anger and forgave his tormentor. In the process, Eddie helped to heal his own deep wounds. "The Bible tells us that our unforgiveness binds us to the person who offended us," Eddie explains. "Just being able to see my uncle as a person helped me understand that what he had done to me was likely the result of what had been done to him. I was better able to let it go after that. And I was thankful that God had brought us together, because on that day the child in my heart that had been held captive for so long was set free to become the man God intended me to be."

Tears of Joy

The first time I heard Eddie Coronado sing was several years ago at Christ For The Nations Institute in Dallas, where he was on the school's main worship team. He sang a duet with a young lady, and I marveled at his beautiful voice. As a singer I notice individual voices, and Eddie's stood out on so many levels.

Again the Lord's plan was at work, because when it came time to put together a worship team with a band and singers at Daystar, I immediately thought of Eddie and his beautiful voice, so filled with a sound of hope. I mentioned Eddie to David Ribb, our director of audio at Daystar. He made it his mission to find Eddie.

David came back a few days later and said that he'd found Eddie living just a few miles from our headquarters at the time. We invited Eddie for a meeting, and from the first time he walked into the studio, I knew it was a divine connection—and that Eddie was going to bless the world with his singing in both English and Spanish. (Eddie will tell you that his native tongue is "the language of heaven.")

Today Eddie and Valarie have a teenage son, whom they dote upon. Eddie has performed on more than twenty albums in English and Spanish. He hopes someday to go back to the now-shuttered El Paso church and The Upper Room where he was saved and rebuild it so that he might help other young people find their way to the Lord. "That would complete the circle," Eddie told me.

And though he remains a modest man, Eddie has become a powerful voice at Daystar, not just in his singing but also in his incredible testimony, which continues to touch the hearts of millions of people. Eddie can break your heart with his stories—and he can make you laugh. He relates that he was called to the principal's office so much in his school days that he still gets nervous when his name is called over the intercom at Daystar. "It's like, what did I do now? Am I in trouble again?" he says laughingly.

"I look back at my life in East L.A. and on the streets of Juarez and now at where the Lord has brought me, and I can't believe it. God continues to show me that He has even more plans for my life. I know that He is real because of everything I have been through and where I am today."

3

Surrender Your Marriage

arcus and I have been married twenty-five years. In all that time, we've never had a fight or even a minor disagreement. And if you believe that, I have some waterfront land in the Mojave Desert I'd like to sell you.

If ever there is a place where the act of surrender is required, it is in the institution of marriage. Surrendering your self-interests and your self-centeredness to a loving, lifelong relationship can be one of the great gifts of a lifetime, but it isn't always easy. Every couple has challenges. Every husband and every wife has to make adjustments and compromises to keep the relationship on track. Marriage is not a fifty-fifty deal; it demands that each person give 100 percent.

One out of every two marriages ends in divorce. And that's only part of the story. Many more marriages suffer from neglect, abuse, dishonesty, and cheating. So many forces are at work to tear at the fabric of a marriage. Talk to any veteran married couple, and they'll readily agree that each marriage faces significant challenges. These challenges include such issues as how to put God first in the marriage, effective communication, child-rearing views, money management, and many more. In all of these areas, it is crucial for couples to search for God's will together.

Here are ten challenges I put at the top of the list:

1. Putting God first in the marriage
2. Managing money and financial pressures
3. Communicating effectively and resolving conflict
4. Being in agreement on how to raise children
5. Putting your spouse before your children
6. Dealing with addictions (drugs, alcohol abuse, pornography)
7. Maintaining a healthy sex life
8. Learning to forgive one another
9. Handling health issues
10. Balancing schedules

Before You Say "I Do"

I wish more men and women would stop and consider the challenges of marriage before taking their vows. It could make their marriages stronger and even save them great grief down the road. No couple wants to focus on potential problems or throw the proverbial wet blanket over wedding plans, but premarital counseling can be enjoyable and enlightening when done correctly. Marcus and I did not have premarital counseling, but we would have greatly benefited from sitting down with a pastor or counselor to discuss our long-term goals, personality conflicts, and family issues to be certain that we were both on the same page and to talk about adjustments we would have to make.

Far too many couples are naive in thinking that marriage will solve problems in a relationship or that once the vows are said it is possible to "fix" a spouse. That is not the case. Once you are married, the greatest impact you can have is to live a surrendered life so that your spouse can witness the benefits and, hopefully, decide to do the same. Only God, the One who so intricately designed and fashioned us, has the tools to fix people.

I've heard people joke that husbands and wives should come with an operator's manual. Believe it or not, there is one. It's called the Bible. When we follow the Lord's words and surrender fully to Him and pray, He can fix anything. It might not happen as quickly as you or I would like because the Lord works in His own time frame, but a surrendered and yielded life will give God the opportunity to heal the hurts, repair what is broken, and apply forgiveness as the ultimate finish.

Communication

Since Marcus and I work as broadcasters and we each host television shows, you'd think that communication would be a strong point in our relationship. We don't have a problem expressing ourselves, but communication works both ways—talking and listening; and like most couples, we've had to remind ourselves of that from time to time.

The first year of marriage was glorious but challenging for us because both Marcus and I have strong personalities. At first we butted heads because he'd stick to his opinions and I'd stick to mine. We were two separate human beings before becoming one as man and wife. We each had our own ideas on how our marriage would unfold. Both of us are strong willed.

We gradually learned that it took a lot less energy to compromise and focus on areas where we agreed rather than those where we did not agree.

We learned to set boundaries and discuss the disagreements or problems until a solution could be agreed upon.

We also had different methods for dealing with the inevitable conflicts and clashes. Marcus wants to hash things out, and I tend to run from disagreements. Plus, Marcus didn't grow up with sisters, so he really thought he'd hooked up with an alien life form when we settled into our marriage; he had a hard time with the contrast in the "emotional" versus "logical" take on things.

We had to find an approach that worked for both of us. We had to make adjustments. We each had to learn that seeking to "win" marital disagreements was the wrong approach. Understanding is far more important. I learned that sometimes I just had to let my spouse claim victory, knowing that by so doing we would share the ultimate victory of a peaceful relationship.

Time Together

To communicate effectively, Marcus and I have to be together. I've found that Marcus needs my time, my attention, and my affection. When he has that, he is fulfilled and he is happy and able to lead our family as the godly husband God intended him to be. I'm the same way.

At times, though, we did not make our marriage our top priority. I got busy taking care of kids and others and doing my own daily TV show. Marcus got busy with running the ministry that was growing bigger day by day. How many marriages have crumbled because two people have grown apart? We don't want that to happen. Our individual responsibilities have grown as our ministry has grown. We've both had to learn to say no to people who want our time, because it would take us away from each other. I've had to turn down speaking engagements and other opportunities that would pull me away from my family, and so has Marcus. We've learned to put each other always at the forefront.

Recently we even rededicated ourselves to each other; we reaffirmed that next to our relationship with the Lord, our marriage comes first. We decided to save Saturdays for "us." It struck us that there needed to be at least one day when our focus was on each other. No shopping. No golf. No slipping into the office just to catch up on a few things. Text messaging and e-mailing doesn't do it for us. We need time alone together to affirm each other and to affirm our commitment to each other as a couple in God's eyes. This has been an amazing adjustment for us, and our marriage is stronger today than it ever has been.

Marcus uses our alone-together time each evening to read the Scriptures, and we take turns praying for each other. One of my favorite moments of each day is when we wake up, cuddle together, and Marcus prays for us. That old cliché you've heard many times is really true: "The couples that pray together, stay together." Prayer focuses us on each other and God's presence in our marriage, and it seems to help keep each of us on track throughout the day when challenges and distractions arise. We enjoy the intimacy of reconnecting in prayer together each morning and evening. We discuss our days, the kids, our plans for the future. We even lock the door so our teenage kids know that we need some private time together.

We also lock the door because, yes, it's important to have a healthy sex life. God designed sex and meant it to be enjoyed and fulfilling for both husband and wife. So if you're not connecting sexually, that's not a healthy marriage. Next to your relationship with God, your marriage takes precedence and meeting one another's needs is vital. When a husband and wife are connected spiritually, physically, and emotionally, you have a marriage that can stand the test of time. With God as the center and both individuals surrendered to Him, you can overcome anything.

In-Laws

Marriage goes beyond two people saying vows. Marcus told me that when he was dating as a single minister, he always took into consideration the families of the girls and whether he was compatible with them, too. I don't think couples realize that when you marry someone, you also marry that person's family. Marcus shied away from a couple of girls he liked because he could tell that their families would not be supportive of a minister's life or there were family issues that would have posed problems to a marriage.

Having good relationships with the in-laws is important. Anyone who has had conflicts in that arena will tell you that bad relationships with in-laws can be a nightmare. Your spouse's family members will be a significant part of your relationship, good or bad. If you see signs of trouble before the marriage, I'd advise you to address those problems before you get married, or at least consider the consequences.

When we started dating, Marcus hit it off with my family. I think they might have loved him even before I did. My parents approved of our dating relationship and felt very good about us being together. It was such a blessing for me to have my parents' approval. Now that I'm a parent, I realize that God gives us a great sensitivity toward those who will be good partners for our children. Our parents want the best for us, and they know us well enough to understand our strengths and weaknesses—and what sort of person will be good for us in the long term.

The first time Marcus took me to meet his family in Macon, Georgia, we got in late and they were already in bed. The next morning I was asleep in my room when Marcus and his mother peeked in on me. He told me later that, as his mother looked at me, Marcus said, "Mama, isn't she beautiful?" That still warms my heart. And it was a good sign. I've always found that men who care about their mothers and what they think tend to be very good husbands.

Marcus has always loved and admired his mom. They would sit up for hours and talk about the things of the Lord; she is an important part of who he is today. His dad, a godly man who believed in working hard and doing the right thing, is also important to him. I don't feel like a daughter-in-law in his family, and I never have. They have treated me like a daughter, and my parents have treated Marcus like a son.

On the other side of the coin, if you are married and you don't get along with your in-laws, my advice to you is simple: Honor your spouse's parents. Be intentionally kind, gentle, loving, and patient. One of the Ten Commandments is to "honor your father and your mother" (Exodus 20:12). There is a definite blessing attached to those who honor their parents. God didn't say, "Honor them if they are righteous" or "Honor them if they are good." No, God said, "Honor them" because you cannot imagine what honor and love will do for those hard-case in-laws.

Again, these are spiritual laws to live by, and they may not make any sense in the natural world, not at first. But if you surrender those in-laws to the Lord, honor them, and love them unconditionally, you will eventually see a change. The change might be only in you because you're being obedient to what God is asking you to do. You will be the one who will experience peace, and God can work on your behalf because you're not angry, bitter, and unforgiving. You will be making the choice to love and honor—and God will bless your efforts beyond what you can imagine.

Baggage

My parents acted as talent scouts to help me find Daystar singer Dan Smiley. Dan was leading worship at my parents' church, and my dad described him as having one of the greatest voices he'd ever heard. Soon after that, my daughter Rachel attended a service at their church and came home talking about the wonderful voice of the worship leader. But what stood out the most to her was his sincerity in his singing to the Lord. That combination of sincerity and dedication to God makes for a beautiful sound that is not of this world. I wasn't looking for another male vocalist for Daystar, but I had to go hear this guy for myself after all of the family testimonials. I attended a service and immediately understood what my daughter and parents had recognized—something special.

I invited Dan to sing with the Daystar group at our annual Refreshing Times Women's Conference, and he fit right in. We knew then that Dan was meant to be a part of our group. Since that time, Dan has joined the singers who travel with me and my husband as we minister to conferences and churches. He also sings nearly every day on the live *Celebration* program televised around the world by Daystar. "I'm living my dream," Dan told me.

But Dan's life was not always a dream. Dan is the youngest of eight children from a broken family. When he was just six years old, his father left their mother to live with another woman. "He was a very affectionate and tender man," Dan says, "but also very strong. I really loved him. He would walk us to school and come home from work and give us change for the ice-cream man. When he left, I took it pretty hard. My whole world crashed." Dan still loved his dad and wasn't mad at him, but he didn't understand.

Dan's mother was a Christian who preached and served as an evangelist. She tried to ground her children in church youth activities and the choir. "My mom did everything she could to keep us out of trouble, but it was very challenging in South Miami."

Dan grew up with God in his life and even felt called to preach at the age of sixteen, but he denied that call. "I argued against it saying that I wanted to experience more before I gave myself to the Lord," he says. "I told God that if He let me do my own thing until I was thirty that I would preach for Him. I just wanted to explore the world. I thought it was harmless."

After Dan had his first sexual experience, he became promiscuous. "That failure in my father fell over onto me," he admits. "I was searching for approval and attention that I never got from my father, so I sought it from women."

At the age of nineteen, Dan met Tamar and married her four months later. But he was not faithful to her, even after they started a family. "The seed of unfaithfulness was still on me—that flaw in my character. It was still there. I couldn't shake it," he says.

God did not give up on Dan, even when Dan turned his back on Him. At the age of thirty, he returned to church with his wife and children—and felt a powerful presence come over him once again. "The Word was being preached at the service, and it hit me like a ton of bricks. I fell to my knees and I felt the presence of the Lord," Dan recalls. "I was arrested by the Holy Spirit, and God reminded me of the promise I had made at sixteen. I rededicated my life to the Lord."

Even then, however, Dan struggled to live up to his promises. For two more years, he wrestled with the demons of infidelity. He had an affair with a married woman—and thereby put his family in jeopardy. The woman's husband sent two armed men to Dan's house to teach him a lesson. They came to the Smiley family home with a gun and a baseball bat. They forced his wife and children to watch as they attacked Dan in their living room. Dan fought back, grabbing the bat away from one of them. After a long struggle he escaped out the front door and ran to a neighbor's home to call the police. The attackers fled and were never heard from again.

"I hit bottom," admits Dan. "I'd put my family in jeopardy, and it was horrible and scary. I told the Lord I'd had enough." He prayed to God and committed his life to Him. "I finally got serious about my surrender. And once I did that, everything changed."

Dan had to make things right with his wife and sons. He had to apologize to them and start over to prove his worth as a husband and father. Dan continues, "The beautiful thing is that the Lord will allow you to be redeemed once you truly surrender."

Dan came to realize that surrender is willingly giving over the complete control of your life to the Lord. "That takes a lot of faith and trust. For me, surrender was a very challenging thing because I try to control every aspect of my life. Surrendering was like putting on blinders, falling backward, and believing that God was not going to let my head hit the floor."

Dan has been a Daystar singer for more than five years now, and he acknowledges that surrender is a daily effort. "I have no idea where I am going. I walk one step at a time, and I believe the next step is the right one because I trust in the Lord's plan," he says. "That is a challenge for me to do. Every day, I try to make sure that I listen to the Holy Spirit, and whatever way He says I should go, I go that way."

One of the most interesting parts of Dan's story is that during all those years of living life the way he wanted, he dreamed about being an international singing star. He didn't succeed. "Then I gave that dream up to the Lord," Dan says, "and it took Him less than two years to bring me to Daystar, something I had failed to accomplish in seventeen years on my own."

From Dan's experience, we are reminded that God always has a plan waiting for each and every one of us. Dan thought he had blown his opportunity. He never imagined he would have the chance to sing to the world. Today he is extremely grateful to be sharing his message of hope. His surrender changed his life dramatically in many ways.

Serving Each Other

One of my mentors, Bunny Wilson, says that many married women have it backward: they serve their children and teach their husbands. We should be serving our husbands and teaching our children. If we are good to our spouses in front of our children, that will make the biggest impression in their lives. If we are rude and indifferent to our spouses, our children will likely follow that pattern in their own relationships.

Next to God, our spouses come first, then our children, our churches, jobs, and outside activities. That's easier said than done. Children don't just want our attention, they demand it. Obligations, especially honorable ones, can easily distract us.

Our carnal flesh is concerned about our needs, our wants, and our desires. But, as we surrender to our Creator and follow His wisdom as laid out in the Word of God, we understand that our fleshly selves are at war with our spiritual selves. We must build up our spiritual selves to survive in marriage. What does that mean? It means responding in a way that is opposite of the desires of our flesh. Instead of focusing on *our own* needs, wants, and desires, we need to respond to the needs, wants, and desires of our spouses. Choosing each other, showing kindness to each other, and being joyful in the process is critical.

Instead of doing "unto your spouse," you do "unto the Lord." The amazing thing is that when you honor your spouse out of your love for

God, your marriage is enriched—because you aren't seeking affirmation from your husband or wife, you are seeking it from the Lord.

We are spiritual beings, and so when we look to people to fulfill our needs we are always disappointed. But when we look to God to meet our needs, we are truly fulfilled and blessed. People will let us down, but our Lord will never leave us nor forsake us. One of my favorite passages from Scripture is "I am with you always, even to the end of the age" (Matthew 28:20). To me, that means we are never alone, and no matter what situations we face, God will see us through. Even if our spouse doesn't surrender to the Lord's will, God will continue to work in our lives. We do not have to be afraid.

Forgiveness

Forgiveness is a powerful healing balm for married couples. Without forgiveness, your marriage can easily become too painful to bear. Forgiveness is liberating. It sets you free. I know of an unfaithful husband who had a single one-night stand while drinking heavily. He was extremely remorseful. His wife decided to stay with him, but she found it difficult to forgive him. She tried to contain her anger rather than exploding at him, but then it ate at her from within, causing intense stress, anxiety, and health problems. When we refuse to forgive others, we risk our own well-being.

Finally, she told a visiting speaker at her church that she was having a hard time forgiving her husband. The speaker offered wise counsel. "What has God forgiven you? Remember what you have been forgiven, and you will be able to forgive your husband." His words set her free. When she pondered the many mistakes she had made in her life, she realized that if God had forgiven her, she could surely forgive her husband.

I'm not suggesting that continued sin against each other in a marriage can always be resolved. But I do believe that many marriages can be salvaged, and it always starts with forgiveness. God hates divorce (see Malachi 2:16), and He makes it possible to move past any and every challenge through forgiveness. God can heal and restore all hearts. God is omniscient; He knows exactly how you're feeling. God is omnipotent; He has all power to heal and restore. God is omnipresent; He is present even in your marriage.

Before You Say "I Don't"

One of the things I have learned from the guests on our shows and from the mail and phone calls we receive is that no marriage is beyond repair, no wrong beyond restoration, and no mistake too big to be forgiven. God's grace covers us all. We love sharing stories of redemption on our show, and it is good to understand that we all have struggles and dark times. Even great leaders of the faith struggle in their marriages.

My friend Rhonda Davis, founder of the Hadassah School of Ministry in Cleveland, Tennessee, has talked openly on my show about the challenges she and her husband, Hank, have overcome in their marriage. It is truly one of the most awesome stories of redemption, grace, and mercy I've ever heard in this context.

Rhonda grew up in a minister's home with loving parents. She calls it a *Leave It to Beaver* idyllic childhood, but one steeped in faith. Her goal was to be "God's girl and to serve Him." As a teenager she fell in love with Hank, a handsome California contractor.

Hank was seven years older than she and had briefly dated her older sister—and both her sister and her parents warned Rhonda about him. "He has a past," people said. Rhonda, however, hadn't picked up on any bad signals. She saw Hank as a churchgoing, Christian man who was working hard to build a business while also practicing and living his faith with the Lord. He'd even told her that he'd felt a call to the ministry, and someday he might answer it in a larger way.

They were married in 1979, and the first signs of trouble in their relationship quickly appeared. Hank's life as a Christian deteriorated so rapidly, Rhonda wondered if it had been a charade from the beginning. She discovered that he smoked not only cigarettes but also marijuana. He told her that it helped him deal with the stress of his job and that it was common among construction crews. One addiction leads to another once the Enemy of Christ gets a foothold. Within a few months, Rhonda realized that Hank also was doing cocaine and methamphetamines, known as "crystal meth" or "speed."

Rhonda's charmed existence was imperiled. She prayed that Hank would see the great error of his ways, but his addictions only grew worse. She realized she was married to an addict who was running from the call of God. Like many women, Rhonda blamed herself—she had been a virgin when they married, and she knew Hank was frustrated. She took all the blame for some things that premarital counseling could have helped both Rhonda and Hank work through together—first, not expecting each other to learn the art of lovemaking overnight, and next, how to fulfill each other, something that takes time, patience, and commitment. So while Rhonda blamed herself, Hank chose to move away from her and God and into addiction.

Feeling lost and forsaken, Rhonda prayed, *God, where are You?* "I'd like to say that the heavens opened," she admits, "and that God said 'Here I am,' but nothing happened."

Rhonda no longer recognized the man she'd married. His personality and even his looks had changed because of the drugs. She watched as Hank went through the addict's typical behavior pattern. He would go on a bender, rage at her and deny God's existence, hit bottom, and then re-verse course and beg forgiveness, saying that she was all that he had and that he worshiped her.

Rhonda found herself watching hours of Christian television, trying to immerse herself in her faith and looking for hope. "Marilyn Hickey and other ministers on television and radio would say, 'You can make it no mat-ter what you are facing. Jesus loves you.' And I would hold on to that as if it were a rope extended by God," she says in looking back.

In one dark moment, Rhonda had to go to church to teach a Bible class to children, but Hank was in a stupor from drugs and alcohol and refused to give the car keys to her. It was storming outside, but she walked two miles in a pouring rain to the church.

"I felt so sorry for myself. I was calling out to God: *Where are You? What is going on? Why are You letting this happen?* I was so angry and frus-trated because I felt I'd served Christ all of my life. *What did I ever do to deserve this?*"

During that walk and talk with God, Rhonda said He spoke to her. He promised a miracle but didn't say how or when it would be delivered. With her faith bolstered, Rhonda taught her Bible class and then caught a ride home with some parents. Then she packed her bags and called her mother to come pick her up. She left Hank in his drunken stupor.

Rhonda did not see Hank for two weeks. When she finally went back to get the rest of her stuff, he was a mess—first weeping and then raging and then begging her not to leave. "He started following me around the house saying, 'Please don't leave me.' He put his head on my back and said, 'You are the only one who has ever loved me.'"

Years later, Hank could only recall that he'd reached the lowest of low points. The night before Rhonda returned to get her things, he had taken mescaline, a hallucinogenic derivative of the peyote plant, along with co-caine and alcohol. "I went into the bathroom and my reflection began to melt. Monsters were crawling on the carpet. Rhonda's mother flew in from Tennessee, and when they came that morning to pack up and move out, my brain was fried from drugs and lack of sleep. I wanted to manipulate her. I was trying to get her back, but the Devil was playing games with me."

Hank didn't make it easy for Rhonda to walk away. She was torn by the dying embers of her love for him. But bitterness and rejection also filled her heart. She and her mother left him and went to the airport.

Hank followed them, saying he wanted to carry their bags to the plane. Finally, he begged Rhonda, "If I change, will you come back to me?" Rhonda said yes to appease him, but once in Tennessee, she hired a lawyer and obtained a divorce.

Starting Over

Hank held on to Rhonda's vague promise and used it as his steppingstone back to God. That Sunday night, Hank found himself alone in their house. Somehow, he managed to stay sober. He pulled himself together, despite his anger and despair, and went to church. "It was one of those old-time services where the pastor gave invitations for people to come up and be saved. I knew I needed to go, but I wasn't sure I was ready. This little gray-haired grandmother came up to me and invited me to go up and pray. I shook my head no. But somehow, I found myself at the altar. She had just taken my hand and led me up there. I prayed, *God, if You are real, be real to me now*, and I felt the Holy Spirit come over me."

After the service, Hank walked out to the parking lot and discovered that his car had been repossessed during church. He'd asked God to get real with him, and you don't get much more real than that, do you?

He walked home and found his drug-abusing friends partying there. "I told them that I'd just given my heart to God, and I didn't want any more drugs in my house. Then I went outside and prayed. When I finally went back in the house, I was shocked that they'd taken me seriously. The cocaine, the hash pipes, the water bongs, the roach clips, the wine coolers, and the beer bottles were all gone. They had cleaned the house just as thoroughly as I'd cleaned my soul. It was a miracle. And I never did another drug. I surrendered my heart and my life to God, and I've never smoked another cigarette or had another beer. I just completely walked away—no, I ran away—from that life."

To free himself from the lifestyle of an addict, Hank had to get away from that environment and those people. He started hanging out with people who were health-and-fitness conscious, and he sought out couples who had good healthy marriages so he could learn what that was like too. He even changed the music he listened to because of the many subliminal messages in rock songs dealing with drugs. "Slowly, God began to honor my efforts to be a better man and a better Christian."

God is our Father and we must trust Him. If we choose to behave in a way that pleases Him, we will see that His ways are good. Hank returned to church and his faith, committing himself more than he ever had before. He also transformed his body. "I'd met Mr. Teenage America at a gym, and we began working out together. I got my strength and my weight back up. I even got all of the other young bodybuilders to go to church with me. We sat in the front row and told the preacher that if anybody got out of hand we'd take care of it," he remembers, smiling.

Hank began speaking and evangelizing. In the year that followed, he journeyed to Israel in a group with Marcus and me. We became friends and, of course, we learned of his journey into the depths of despair, his loss of the woman he loved, and his surrender to the Holy Spirit. His body and his soul were healing, thanks to his surrender, but Hank's heart still ached for his former wife.

Rhonda, during this two-year process, wasn't aware of any changes in Hank. When he wrote to her and called her on the telephone, she did not believe that he had changed at all. She was trying to move on with her life. She had enrolled in Lee University to study for the ministry. She even began to date other ministers, but it didn't go well. Several told her she'd be the perfect wife if she hadn't been divorced. One wanted to date her but didn't want to be seen with her by his congregation. Another prayed in front of her saying, "God, do what You can with her, make something of her life." She felt like something pitiful, like damaged goods.

Hank, on the other hand, hadn't given up on her. He knew that God had healed other marriages and held on to the hope that He would heal theirs too. Marcus had known Rhonda before she married Hank, and after their sad divorce, Marcus had been one of the only people to encourage Hank to believe that God could restore their marriage. Everyone else was pretty much telling him to give up. "That light never did burn out," Hank says. "I started studying what it meant to be a good husband. I would never listen to our marriage counselor before—I mostly wanted to beat him up—but once I started reading about how to be a good man and a good husband, I became more determined than ever to get Rhonda back. I just wish I had learned those things before we got married." Finally he went to Tennessee to beg her to come back.

"He looked like Mr. Universe, all buff and tan with a big ol' muscular neck," remembers Rhonda. But after so many lies and disappointments and betrayals, she found it hard to believe that Hank had changed spiritually. "I told him I was glad he got saved, but I wanted to get on with my life."

Hank returned to California, disappointed in his failure to convince Rhonda to return to him. But God's plan often differs from our expectations. He was still working on Hank. When Hank returned to California, the Lord called him to the ministry, and he began traveling around the country preaching the Lord's Word.

Reconciled

Before I had ever met Rhonda, I felt I knew her well because Hank was always talking about her and how he would never love another woman as much as he loved her. They had been divorced for nearly three years, yet he still felt that way about her, and he still wanted to restore their relationship and remarry.

Rhonda was in her third year of studying for the ministry when she heard that Hank was preaching. She didn't want to believe it, but God was asking her to walk in obedience and to trust Him. As she did, Jesus healed her hurt and anger, cleansing the wounds in her soul. "It felt like God was pulling the bitter roots out of me. He asked me to forgive myself and to forgive Hank. I also had to forgive God because I was holding bitterness against Him too. At times it was so difficult, it felt like I had the flu, but God walked me through the healing."

The most difficult part of Rhonda's walk on the Path of Surrender came when she returned, in her mind, to the house that had been home to her troubled marriage. Her most painful memories, conscious and repressed, resided in that house. God knew that she would not be free to live and forgive until the haunting memories within those walls were erased from her mind. "The Lord began to walk me through my house, and I felt the presence of Jesus and I heard him say 'I have come to heal you, Rhonda,'" she recalls. "He opened the door of the house that held horror for me. The memories came at me like scenes from a movie as He walked me around. God said to me, *There is no fear in this room for you because Jesus is Lord of this room.*"

As she mentally stepped through each room of the house and the painful memories they contained, Rhonda felt God's presence and her fears, anguish, and sorrow dissolve. "I felt like a bird that had been let out of a cage," she says. "The Lord said, *I have come today to do what I promised years ago.* He freed me from the darkness, and He walked me through forgiveness."

Rhonda wanted and needed that sense of peace described in Isaiah 48:18, "peace...like a river" and "righteousness like the waves of the sea." God told her that He was going to bring her to a place of rest because she had been wandering lost and ill at ease.

She went to a Christian counselor who told her, "You have to realize that this is something that happened to you, and you are divorced, but you are not permanently scarred by it. You do have a future." Rhonda finally escaped from that stigma of feeling scarred or like a leftover when she surrendered to God's will. She realized that God wants us whole hearted and restored. "He restored me not to put me back with Hank but because I am the Lord's daughter," she says.

Up to that point, Rhonda had not dealt with her past, and she couldn't move into the future. The Holy Spirit led her to a place of divine healing. Then, and only then, did God help Rhonda return to Hank. She felt compelled to talk with him, to let him know she had forgiven him, but she was focused more on getting closure than on reuniting with him. What happened next took her by surprise.

Marcus called Rhonda and told her that Hank had truly changed and that he would be ministering at a church in Georgia. Marcus encouraged her to go and hear Hank preach. Rhonda was not convinced that Hank was called to minister, but she trusted Marcus. Though doubtful, Rhonda decided to make the short drive to the church to hear Hank for herself. He was preaching in Dalton, Georgia, only thirty miles away.

Rhonda was shocked at the sincerity and earnestness in Hank's preaching. Truly, it was a miracle to see what God had done in Hank's life. Rhonda realized the prodigal son had finally come home and surrendered not only to the Lord but also to the call of God on his life. God reunited them and, in that instant, they both felt His presence in their lives.

"Hank looked at me and said, 'You are still my wife,' and the Lord healed my heart. A lightning bolt went from Hank to me and back again, and the heartbreak was over," she remembers.

Rhonda now often ministers to other women who've suffered in bad relationships. She tells them that she and Hank serve as examples that there is always hope. Nothing is impossible with a healing God as long as people are willing to surrender and put their trust in Him.

I don't believe their marriage ever could have been restored if both Hank and Rhonda had not surrendered their relationship to God's will. And I don't believe either of them ever would have been happy married to other people if they hadn't gone through the Path of Surrender. Eighty percent of second marriages fail because people enter into them thinking they are fine, but then they encounter the same issues that ruined their first marriages.

Hank and Rhonda realized they would hold on to those demons unless they acted, so they went back to a marriage counselor. This time, both of them were prepared to listen and learn. "Even today, I know there are things I do that drive Rhonda nuts, but I want her to help me be a better husband," Hank says. "That's what happens when you really get out of yourself and into loving your wife just as Christ loved the church. I want to grow old with her so we can sit on the porch at the end of life and look at our grandkids and say, 'If we made it, you can make it.' I want to know that the Devil went to God and said, 'This is one marriage I didn't destroy.' And then God can say, 'There will be many more that you will not tear apart.'"

In our twenty-five years together, Marcus and I, too, have learned how important it is to forgive one another and to move on. Even today we are still learning to listen to each other, spend time with each other, and to never take each other for granted. Marriage was instituted by God, and He designed marriage to be permanent. I don't condemn anyone who has gone through a divorce, but I think many marriages could be saved by surrendering individual interests for the good of the long-term relationship.

4

Surrender Your Children

Isaiah Reed, who comes from a long line of preachers, was brought up in the church. He was saved and filled with the Holy Spirit at the age of seven.

But the Enemy went to work on this godly child.

Isaiah was lured into gang activity and involved in a drive-by shooting as a teen. He avoided being sent to a juvenile home by going into the military, where he fell into illegal black-market activities while serving overseas. A good organizer with a natural gift for business, Isaiah betrayed his faith and his gifts by using his skills to create an international drug and prostitution ring that continued after he left the military.

If ever there was a mother who surrendered her wayward son to God, it was the mother of Isaiah Reed. His father disowned him when he learned of Isaiah's criminal enterprise, but both parents continued to pray for his salvation.

In the fall of 1986, Isaiah was attacked during a drug deal with Colombian dealers. One of them shot him twice in the face during a struggle in a car. Several others stabbed him sixteen times in the upper body before they threw him out of the car and left him for dead in an alley. As Isaiah fell into a coma, he heard his father's voice say, "You're going to end up in an alley in a puddle of blood by yourself."

Isaiah's mother sensed that something had happened to him even before she learned that he'd been attacked, and she began praying for him.

The rescue squad that found Isaiah couldn't detect any vital signs. They radioed the hospital with a report that they were bringing in a body. When Isaiah's mother was notified that her son was found dead in the street, she said, "I have heard your report. But I got a report right here. Let me read you my report card." She told them that her son was not dead because she believed God was not done with him yet. "God promised me a preacher not a pimp," she insisted.

The doctors still thought Isaiah was dead. He was on an autopsy table, about to be cut open, when a doctor found faint vital signs. Even then, the doctors were convinced that he would be paralyzed the rest of his life from his injuries. Isaiah's mother refused to accept that news. She told the doctors to leave his room while she prayed for him.

A few months later, Isaiah walked out of the hospital. His body was miraculously healed, but his soul was still dark. He returned to his criminal life for three years, despite his mother's prayers.

On December 27, 1989, while doing drugs in a room with his friends in Hawaii, one of the women began screaming. Though he intended to punch her to make her be quiet, he found himself praying for her instead. Suddenly, everyone in the room could feel the presence of the Holy Spirit. Confused, Isaiah prayed to the Lord, "If You're real, come into my life or else I'll kill everyone in this room." Everyone in the room was knocked to the floor by an unseen hand. They all cried and repented, and Isaiah never touched drugs again.

He did, however, still have to face the punishment for his crimes. He was arrested in a raid that day by police who had been watching him. He ended up serving more than three years in prison, and he used his time to get an education and to kick drugs.

Upon his release, he became an associate pastor and started a ministry. Isaiah and his wife, Carol, a former prostitute, now lead Christian Vision Ministries in Richmond, Texas. He preaches that you can't get to heaven on the coattails of your grandmother's or mother's prayers, but having a good prayer warrior on your side certainly can help.

Isaiah explains, "My mother never gave up on me. She believed the Lord. She did not doubt."

A Motherless Child

Not every child is so blessed. One of our Daystar family members, Jennifer Falcon, was two weeks old when she was dropped off at an orphanage near Seoul in Korea. She learned many years later that she was abandoned because her mother was a servant who became pregnant during a liaison with the son of a wealthy landowner descended from royalty.

Jennifer spent fourteen years in the orphanage. She watched children starve. Others committed suicide. She was physically, emotionally, and sexually abused. Fifty kids slept in an eight-by-eleven-foot room. Children were beaten if they didn't read their Bible lessons, which did not seem like a very Christian approach. But Jennifer somehow found it in her heart and soul to pray.

She was thirteen years old when she woke up one morning after having a vision that her prayers were going to be answered and she was going to be adopted. She had feared it would never happen. But a family did choose her. There were four sons in the family; a daughter had passed away, so the parents wanted another one.

This was an American family. Jennifer did not speak English at the time of her adoption, so there were language problems at first. The emotional problems were worse. Jennifer had grown up in hardship. She shied away from human contact. She even found it impossible to sleep on a bed because she'd always slept on the floor. She was afraid she'd fall off the high bed.

At first she was grateful for the regular meals and clothing, but she grew to resent the way her adoptive mother abused her. Jennifer was treated more like a housekeeper than a child. Her brothers went to school, but her mother kept her home to do the housework. She was given lessons to do, but her mother would hit her if they weren't done properly. There were other abuses going on in the household as well.

Jennifer finally reached the age of eighteen and left. With the help of a nurse she had befriended, she got into nursing school. She also married and started her own family. All the while, she wondered who her birth parents were and if she would ever have an opportunity to meet them. At age thirty-three, she began to relearn Korean. She harbored a dream of meeting her birth parents and began to save the money to fly back to her native country. She hoped to not only find her father but also find the mother she had so longed to see—and even as she worked toward her dream, she told God: *I surrender. I want this to happen but I trust you if it doesn't.* It was hard to surrender a lost childhood and then to surrender the hope of finding her parents.

In the end God did what only He could do and brought Jennifer full circle. Jennifer returned to Korea and met the mother who had been forced to give her up. "She just kept touching my face and my hair and crying, and I was so thankful I met her," says Jennifer. Today she is happy, whole, and healed. She has two amazing kids, and you would never know the heartache of her story by looking at the countenance of peace you see on her face.

Teach by Example

I am a product of parents who dedicated and surrendered me to the Lord at an early age. I watched both of my parents follow the Lord and lead upright lives. They taught me and my siblings by example. They worked hard, told the truth, loved unconditionally—and taught us to do the same. They loved God and loved us. My parents provided a strong foundation so that I could go out into the world and flourish. Their love for me has been multiplied, magnified, and spread.

The best way to surrender your children to God is to live a life before them that will cause them to one day put their trust in God. A life surrendered to God and modeled before our children will have an impact on our children's children and, ultimately, affect eternity.

You and I know parenting is not easy. We can't put on the cruise control with kids, because just when we think they are rolling along smoothly toward adulthood, they swerve off the road. Marcus and I have never pretended to be the perfect parents. Parents need to admit to their children that they aren't perfect, that they make mistakes, and that they need God's guidance. Our kids figure it out soon enough, anyway, but we lose credibility with them if we pretend to be infallible.

Marcus and I don't have all the answers when it comes to parenting our children, but we know that God does. We pray for our children, and we pray even more for the Lord's guidance so that we make the right decisions as parents. We are aware that if parents aren't on the same page on how to guide their children, it can cause problems in a marriage. So we work hard at finding solutions together, with God's help.

Mistakes and all, Marcus and I have tried to let our children see the love of God demonstrated in our lives day by day. Our efforts have had a strong impact. I was once shopping in a department store, pushing my three-year-old son in a baby buggy. As I browsed through a clothes rack, he stood up in the buggy. It tumbled over with him in it. Jonathan wasn't hurt, but it scared him so much that he cried out at the top of his lungs: "Pray, Mommy! Pray!"

Even at that young age, Jonathan knew that in times of trouble we pray. I picked him up, returned him to the upright buggy, bent down, and prayed in his ear: "Jesus, help Jonathan to feel better. Amen."

Teach by Your Word

Surrendering your children also requires a willingness to put them in the Word. We made it a point to be in church every Sunday, and children's church was an important part of our kids' lives. Our oldest son, Jonathan, was involved in a group on Wednesday nights that teaches memorizing Scripture verses at an early age. I can remember sitting with him as we would memorize verses from the Bible so he would get his special award at church. I realize that those early years of learning the Bible were so pivotal and would strengthen him for his eventual walk with God.

We sent our two girls to a Christian school that had a required Bible class, and it would always bless me as they quoted entire chapters from the Bible that they had memorized. I know this will serve them well as adults because the Word of God is powerful when it is utilized in our hearts and minds daily. The Word of God says, "Your word I have hidden in my heart, that I might not sin against You" (Psalm 119:11).

When our children were small, we taught them that God has the answer to every question of life. If you have faith in God and a personal relationship with Christ, nothing in your life is too big to overcome through prayer. Children are never too young to learn about surrendering their lives to God. The Bible says that we must become like little children before we can enter the kingdom of God (see Mark 10:15). God loves the faith and heart of little children.

Our youngest, Rebecca, was quite animated as a child. She has a vivid imagination and a gift for exuberant expression. When she was about seven years old, she told me that she had prayed and told God she wanted to see a dolphin at the beach. Her desire to see a dolphin sprang from an annual trip our family makes with my siblings and their families and our parents to Myrtle Beach, South Carolina. We had been going to Myrtle Beach for years, and we had never seen any dolphins, so I was a little concerned that Rebecca might be disappointed. I couldn't tell Rebecca about my doubt and unbelief, so I smiled and agreed with her that when we got to the beach, I would be looking for the dolphins with her.

Of course, Rebecca was positive that God would send dolphins our way. She knew God loved her, and she knew that God could do anything from the stories she had heard from the Bible. So our first morning at the beach house, she was up and eager to get to the water. She ran ahead of us as we walked across the sand, proclaiming that this was the day she would swim with the dolphins. And lo and behold, I looked out across the water and there was an entire school of dolphins leaping in the waves. Now, I'm a big believer in the power of prayer, but I have to admit, I was stunned at this exhibition of it. Rebecca simply took it in stride. She knew God would come through. She surrendered her dream to Him, and He responded. You never know what the Lord's own plan is, but on this day, for this girl, I think He smiled and thought, *Rebecca wants to see My beautiful dolphins, and I'm pretty proud of them, so why not?*

What impressed me the most on that day, and ever since, is the trust that my daughter has in the power of prayer—and all because she took God at His Word.

Give Them Your Time

As a teen, Rebecca was home from school one day and called me at the office.

"Mom, I need to talk to you *right now.*"

Does that sound familiar? If you are a parent, it probably does. Often the temptation for parents—me included—is to resist when we feel our children are feigning urgency just to get our attention. After all, we don't want to spoil them. Sometimes children try to manipulate their parents, and teens often have an urgent need to be at the center of our attention.

I had to make a judgment call. At first I was inclined to brush off my daughter's grab for attention. I told her I had to finish some work before I could come home and talk to her. I heard the disappointment in her voice, and as I put down the phone the maternal instincts kicked into full alert. *She needs me now,* I thought. I stopped what I was doing and called her back to give her the time and attention she needed in that moment. There was no emergency, just as I had thought. But she wasn't manipulating me for attention. She really felt she needed to talk to me about something that was important to her.

Moms and dads are pulled in all directions. We have all these timesaving devices, but I've yet to find any extra hours in my day. Still, when all else fails, I trust my maternal instincts, and on that day they were telling me to tune in to my daughter. Without saying it directly, I was letting her know that she was more important than anything else I was doing at that moment.

Giving up our time for our children is an aspect of surrender that every parent understands. We need to be there for our kids even when it seems as if it doesn't matter, because then they will come to us when it does matter. If we are there for our children when they share everyday experiences—like the difficult science experiment or the mean kid on the bus or the pop quiz that the teacher sprang on them—chances are they will feel they can talk to us later about truly important things, like being pressured to do drugs or have sex.

It would be a mistake to think our children don't notice and appreciate it when we put them at the center of our lives. They can surprise you. Later that same day, Rebecca hugged me and thanked me for "being there."

Giving our time to our children is so important because it develops stronger bonds and opens communication. Parents who put in the time early on will reap the benefits for the rest of their lives. I've yet to meet an elderly person who told me, "I wish I'd spent more time away from my family."

Marcus and I regularly took time away from our television programs so that we could attend school functions and other things important for our kids. We made sure our viewers knew because we wanted to share our priorities with them. Marcus would tell the viewing audience, "Joni isn't here today because the kids have a special event at school, and she didn't want to miss it." We always wanted our kids to know they were more important than our job or even the ministry.

Of course, if I could go back, I would spend even more time with my kids when they were small. I spent a lot of "quality" time with them, but as they get older, I realized that more "quantity" might have been better. Those fleeting moments of childhood are so precious; before you know it, they are grown up and heading out the door to college. Once they are gone, there is no going back.

Kids need to feel that they are at the center of their parents' lives. They want to know they are important to you. I urge all parents—no matter how old their children are—to reach out and tell them you love them. Remember that a loved child becomes a loving spouse and parent. Even if you have not been the perfect parent in the past, remember that children are very forgiving. Once they see that you have reprioritized, they will respond in a positive way.

One way to look at this is to grasp how much our heavenly Father wants to spend time with us. He longs for a personal one-on-one relationship with us. We are His children and He loves us so much; just as He loves us, so must we emulate that same love to our earthly children.

Let Them Go

I once thought that when my children got older, it would be easier. Silly me! I've come to understand that it is easier to be the parent of small children because when they are younger, they are easier to guide—especially when Mom is pushing the baby buggy. It's not so easy when they've got the car keys.

Teenagers are amazing and wondrous to behold—and incredibly challenging. I liken the teen years to a later-stage "terrible twos." Like babies who have moved from crawling to walking, teens get the car keys and decide they are free to go wherever they want to go and do whatever they want to do. They want to make their own decisions, and often we must let them because they need to learn from their own mistakes. We have to stand back, gently guide them, and pray they will remember what we have taught them.

Our middle daughter, Rachel, tested our parental powers when she was dating a young man we didn't approve of. He wasn't a bad kid, but he had addictions and he wasn't making the right choices. Naturally, as parents, we wanted to protect our daughter. The instinct is to go to the rescue, grab your child, and get her out of harm's way. But with teens you have to surrender that instinct. You have to offer your guidance and support but let them make their own choices.

Teens are adults in training, but they usually feel they've already crossed over into adulthood. They look in the mirror and they see adults. Often they are taller than their parents, and most of the time, they are dead certain they are smarter than their parents. They want respect. They want to feel they are in control of their lives. This is part of the maturation process that we all go through. Wise parents adapt. We can't force our belief systems on our children. That will only bring resentment. We try to serve as good examples to them and hope that the Christian foundations we built for them hold up. Parents can and should give advice and encouragement, and they should reinforce the fact that they, more than any others, want the best for their children.

With Rachel we did a lot of encouraging and supporting and reinforcing, believe me. We prayed and at times anguished over the situation. In the end, though, surrendering and trusting God to show her the truth made the difference. Rachel had to see for herself that this boy wasn't the best choice for her—and she did. She saw that they were unevenly yoked. He didn't want to follow the Christian life she aspired to lead. It happened when she returned from a mission trip to Africa, where she visited twenty-eight orphanages. Rachel was deeply touched by the suffering of those parentless children and announced that one day she wanted to build an orphanage of her own.

Give Them to God

Surrendering our children to God may be the most difficult surrender of all. I remember that the day our firstborn, Jonathan, came into the world, I was immediately overcome with intense love for him. And I felt an equal intensity for each of my girls. The love we have for our children cannot be matched. We all want the best for our children. How are we supposed to surrender them?

When I think on this question, I think about my precious mother and how she had to surrender her second child to the Lord. I am her oldest child; I was four years old when my mother gave birth to her second child, a boy born with an open stomach. He survived one week.

My dad told me they covered his tummy with a blanket and he looked just like all the other babies in the nursery. He was beautiful.

But 1960s technology didn't allow a surgery that would have saved his life.

My mother and dad had to surrender that child to the Lord, and even though I didn't understand what had happened, my mother told me later that I would question her about where my baby brother was. She said it was a difficult thing to go through, but she never lost her faith in God, and two years later she would be blessed with another son, Rusty, who looked almost identical to the son who had passed.

Each of us in my family knows that we will see our brother one day in heaven, but in the meantime, surrender is all one can do and trust God to see us through. We don't always understand everything, but that's okay because our trust is in the One who holds tomorrow in His hands.

And so when my own Jonathan was born, and eventually our two girls, I remember thinking that this must be how our heavenly Father loves us. Actually, though, we need to remember that God loves us even more than we love our children—and He loves our children even more than we do.

The Ultimate Surrender

We tend to forget how difficult it must have been for our heavenly Father to let His Son suffer. I cannot fathom a love great enough that would convince me to give the life of my only son. And yet, that is what God did for us. He willingly gave the life of His Son so that all of mankind could receive forgiveness and eternal life. I think about the scene in the movie *The Passion of the Christ,* where a single tear from heaven falls to the ground as God beholds His only Son being crucified. If God could love us that much, then how much more should we be willing to surrender our lives to Him, knowing that He will never leave us and never forsake us.

The Father's Love for His Son

Pastor David Wilkerson of Times Square Church says that a surrendered life is the "act of giving back to Jesus the life He granted you." That decision is significant. However, the surrender that God made is ultimate: the Father sent His only Son to die in our place. When we accept Jesus Christ as our Lord and Savior and surrender to God's will, we reap the rewards of all of His grace.

This is an incredible and wonderful opportunity, yet it is often difficult for people to grasp. The Reverend Bruce Fiol, former senior pastor at Marco Presbyterian Church on Marco Island in Florida, tells a story that helps us understand this concept.

Years ago there was a wealthy industrialist who shared with his son a passion for fine art. The two traveled the world to collect masterpieces by the world's finest artists including Picasso, van Gogh, and Monet. Together they assembled a collection with a value exceeding a billion dollars. The father took pride in his son's appreciation of great art.

The son had also developed a deep sense of duty and patriotism for his country. He was called to serve in time of war, and he answered that call. Just a few weeks after he was deployed to a war zone, the son was reported missing in action. The father's worst fears were confirmed a few days later: his son was killed while rescuing and carrying a wounded soldier to safety. The father mourned his son and fell into a deep grief. He was haunted even by the great works of art that hung in his home because they stirred memories of traveling with his lost child.

One day a young soldier came to his door. He explained that he was the wounded man who had been rescued and carried to safety by the son. The son's friend told of the other lives the son had saved and of the respect that he commanded among his fellow soldiers. "I was your son's friend," the soldier finally said. "We shared a love of art. To honor the memory of my friend, your son, I painted this portrait of him to give to you."

The portrait was no match for the masterpieces that filled the father's home, but it was obviously created with great love. The father placed it over his fireplace as his most beloved painting.

Six months later, the father, weakened by his loss, became ill and died.

The man had no heirs, and his artwork was to be auctioned off. This was one of the most vaunted art collections ever assembled, and people gathered from around the world to make their bids. To everyone's astonishment, the first work presented for sale was not a masterpiece, but the soldier's portrait of the son killed at war. Some of the collectors scoffed when they saw the portrait being brought up and called for another painting, but the auctioneer didn't budge. Instead he informed them that the wealthy man's will clearly stated that no other painting was to be sold until this one was.

The auctioneer called for bids on the portrait, but no one spoke up. He initially called for a starting bid of $10,000. Soon he was imploring the audience for at least a $100 bid.

Finally a family friend offered $100, saying that it was a good likeness of a good man and he would be glad to have it. The auctioneer lifted his gavel, "Going once, going twice, gone." Cheers of relief filled the room. The collectors who had come from museums and private galleries around the globe were eager to finally begin bidding on the masterpieces they had targeted.

But to their amazement, the auctioneer announced the end of all bidding. "According to the will of the father, whoever takes his son gets all that he owns," the auctioneer said.

And so it is with God. Whoever accepts His Son, Jesus Christ, through surrender to Him, will reap all of His Father's blessings.

Surrender Your Career

rancine Rivers grew up in a Christian home, but for many years she didn't live a Christian life. "I went to church, but I didn't realize I needed a Master as well as a Savior," she says. "I thought I was a Christian, but I was not born again, nor did I understand what God's love really is." Still, life seemed to be going well for her. She married a man she had known since the fifth grade. They were good friends in high school and had dated while she was in college and he was in the Marine Corps. They married after she graduated, and they had three children. She also had a successful career, writing "steamy" romance novels for the general market. "Success was all I cared about," she admits. "I was master of my life. *Obey* was a four letter word to me. I'd even had it cut out of my wedding vows."

But Francine could not shake a sense that something was missing. She and her husband, Rick, started a business together, and things began to sour between them. "We made outside changes but nothing on the inside," she says. They had tried a number of churches over the years but never found one where they were truly comfortable. Then, as they were unloading and moving into a new home north of San Francisco in Sebastopol, California, a neighborhood child invited them to his church. Francine, who was still searching to fill a void that she could not identify, felt compelled to try the church. "When I walked in, sat down, and listened, I felt I had come home. Hearing Scripture read and taught changed my life from the inside out. I began to drink the Word." She finally understood that she could not find what was missing in her life until she abandoned her driving desire to be in control. "No change happened for me until I was ready to surrender," Francine explains.

When you feel something is missing, it is because there really is a void. But many of us are like Francine. We are stubborn and resist the truth for far too long before we face the truth and welcome change.

Within a short time, Francine and Rick opened their home to a Bible study group. Not long after that, in May 1986, they were baptized together. When she became a born-again Christian, Francine wanted to share her faith with others but was fearful of offending those who didn't share her new belief in Jesus as Lord and Savior. She was ashamed and frustrated by those conflicting feelings. "I went on a quest, seeking the faith of a martyr. I learned that courage is not something we can manufacture by our own efforts. But when we surrender wholeheartedly to God, He gives us the courage to face whatever comes. He gives us the words to speak when we are called to stand and voice our faith." Francine discovered that surrender is just the first step. God unfolds His plan at His own pace, according to His wisdom, not our schedules.

Francine embraced her Christian beliefs, but she was unwilling to give up her successful career as a writer of steamy historical romances. Then God stepped in as her editor. "Suddenly, nothing I wrote made sense," she recalls. For nearly three years, she had writer's block. "It was a real strange experience to say, 'Lord, You have control over my life,' and then *wham!* that door—writing—is closed."

Looking back, she believes God was refocusing her talents on Him and His Word. Sensing that, she prayed and focused on the Bible, reading through it each year during that period. While reading the book of Hosea, Francine says, "The last defenses I had raised against Jesus's lordship of my life crumbled. The prophet's story broke my heart. I was amazed at how much God loved me, how much He loves each one of us."

It struck her then that writing had become an idol to her. She discovered that when she wrote to glorify Jesus rather than herself, the words again flowed. With her total surrender came the feeling that it was time to return to writing but with a new muse, Jesus. Francine explains, "This time the romance was all about His love for each of us."

With the Lord guiding her writer's voice, Francine redrafted the biblical story of Gomer and Hosea during the time of the California Gold Rush and created what is widely regarded as a masterpiece of Christian literature. It is one of the most powerful and inspiring books I have ever read. *Redeeming Love,* Francine's "statement of faith," has been a perennial best-seller, launching a new, even greater writing career.

"After *Redeeming Love,* the door to writing opened again," she says. "But everything is different now. I measure my success as a writer not in terms of dollars and print runs, but in terms of whether I am following God and using my talents to serve Him. Then, I trust, He will take whatever I do and use it for His purposes."

Francine's award-winning novels have been translated into over twenty different languages, and she enjoys best-seller status in many foreign countries including Germany, the Netherlands, and South Africa. Her writings have inspired millions of Christian readers—including myself.

Francine still considers herself a struggling Christian, fraught with faults and failures. "Writing made me face my own numerous deficiencies and the need to allow Christ absolute sovereignty in all areas of my life. Without Jesus I can do nothing. With Him all things are possible."

Her greatest hope is that her books will encourage other Christians struggling with the same issues that troubled her. She wants her books to be used as tools to present the gospel to unsaved friends and family members. "There are so many people who would rather die than pick up a Bible. Fiction can serve in a nonthreatening way to open minds and, I hope, hearts to the Word of God." Francine surrendered and found inspiration from the Lord. The old Francine was driven by her own ego; now she is driven by a godly force as He directs her on His chosen path.

Balance

For many years women, even in developed nations, had no choice when it came to the direction of their lives. They were not welcome in the workplace, and so the great majority stayed home with their children or held low-level jobs. Wars pulled millions of men out of the work force and, in their absence, women were drawn in. Slowly, economic and social factors changed dramatically. Women were able to move up into management-level positions that paid more but also demanded much more of their time.

Now, many women feel they must choose between work and family. Certainly there are "supermoms" who somehow manage to be strong presences in both places, but even many of them struggle with guilt in both roles. Women who work often feel guilty when they are not home. Women who stay home often feel guilty they aren't bringing in income or pursuing their careers or callings.

This issue affects men too, of course. The demands of the workplace take them away from their wives and children, forcing them to miss things they would rather not miss. Some men whose wives work feel guilty that they can't support the family on their own.

Most of us, men and women, struggle to find a balance and do what works best for our families and our situations when it comes to our careers. There are no easy answers, and one family's solution rarely works for another because of their different circumstances. I have the greatest respect for stay-at-home moms who dedicate their lives to their children. I know they make sacrifices, just as many working mothers and fathers do.

God has given me an opportunity to work outside the home in Christian television, but I do my best to make sure my calling never overrides my first responsibility, which is to my family. Do I always succeed? No. Is it often a struggle? Yes.

Thankfully, we can balance both career and family, but only if we surrender our careers to God. He can show us the paths to follow. He gives divine direction. He opens us to insights. He creates opportunities so that we can take care of our families financially, physically, emotionally, and spiritually.

When we surrender our careers to God, we open ourselves to His innovative and creative plans that can help us overcome even the greatest challenges—and that includes those who are divorced and trying to provide properly for their families as single parents. The Lord can help you find a career path that allows you to survive and thrive in a world that may seem determined to break you and cast you into the gutter.

Faith Integration

The key to success at work is total surrender to God's will, just as Jesus did when He came to do His Father's will on earth. The Son surrendered His life and His will to God's plan for our redemption.

To surrender your career to the Lord is to relinquish control and to submit to God's power and authority, just as Jesus surrendered to His own Father's will. For instance, you may have a job that's fulfilling and that's great, but what if you have a job that's not fulfilling? Can you still be faithful in what God has entrusted to you? Did you ever consider that this might be a season when He wants to teach you and train you for a future job that will be fulfilling? You can simply trust Him with the job that you've been given, knowing this probably isn't your final destination.

I experienced such a thing. Remember the engineering firm I mentioned working for in my early twenties? Well, before that I worked as a waitress. I was faithful to both positions, and I learned a lot in both seasons of my life. To this day, I appreciate any waiter or waitress—and I'm grateful for the service and mindful of how hard some people must work to earn a living. I also enjoy the secretarial skills I learned while working at the engineering firm. Those jobs were not my final destinations as far as a career was concerned, but I remained faithful and steadfast, doing my best, and eventually God opened another door of opportunity.

As you pray and surrender your career, asking for divine direction, you will be amazed at how God will respond with open doors, favor, and divine appointments. He gets the glory for making a way, and you are fulfilled in being exactly where you know the Lord wants you to be.

Some may say that there is no room for God in our work lives—that we should keep our faith and our career separate. But that is an outmoded way of thinking. No less a secular institution than the *New York Times* recognized this in a 2004 Sunday magazine story, which recognized that Christians have always expressed our "Faith at Work," and even more are doing it today. The magazine story, by Russell Shorto, notes that "thousands of businesses...from one-man operations to global corporations to divisions of the federal government, have made room for Christianity on the job, and in some cases have oriented themselves completely around Christian precepts."

Given the problems that immoral business practices have caused in recent years, all Christians should be encouraged to openly surrender their careers and to practice their faith every day of the week, every place they live, work, and play. One example of this cited in the *New York Times* article was "a way station for Christ"—the Riverview Community Bank in Otsego, Minnesota.

One of the fastest-growing start-up banks in the country, Riverview markets itself as a Christian financial institution. A Bible is buried in the foundation of the home office to symbolize that this would be an institution built on righteousness, truth, and integrity. The words "In God We Trust" are engraved in the bank's cornerstone. But most importantly, bank president Chuck Ripka often prays with his customers and co-workers, surrendering to God's wisdom so that he offers the best financial advice and leads the bank successfully. He says Jesus Christ has blessed them because they are obedient to His will.

Ripka believes in spreading God's Word beyond church and into the marketplace, where people spend their daily lives. The bank president told the magazine that he sometimes slips and says to people, "Come on over to the church—I mean the bank." He's not literally a man of the cloth. The writer called him "a marketplace pastor, one node of a sprawling, vigorous faith-at-work movement."[1]

When you surrender in your work or career—whatever "market-place" you labor in—it also makes you eligible for one of the greatest of all benefits: God's helping and healing hands. No situation is beyond repair when you put the Lord first—ahead of your job, your salary, your calling, your ambition, and your ego. When God is allowed first place in your life, no matter the circumstance, He can and will make a way where there seems to be no way. He will never leave you nor forsake you (see Hebrews 13:5).

The Surprise in Surrender

Freda and Gordon Lindsay's story shows how surrendering career and calling allows you to follow God's plan for us.

In 1970 Freda and her husband, Gordon, announced the founding of Christ For The Nations Institute, a Dallas-based Bible school that gathers students both nationally and internationally. Gordon had envisioned "thousands of Spirit-filled believers going forth to do exploits for God around the world."

Born in Zion City, Illinois, in 1906, Gordon was converted to Christianity as a young man, and he came to believe that prayer was as essential as breathing. His parents were disciples of Alexander Dowie, who is considered the father of healing revivalism in America. Gordon's family moved to Portland, Oregon, in his youth. There he was converted and, at the age of eighteen, began his ministry as a traveling evangelist. He conducted meetings for Assembly of God churches and other Pentecostal groups.

At the start of World War II, Gordon was called to become pastor of a church in Ashland, Oregon. He began publishing *The Voice of Healing* in 1948 to cover revivals, evangelists, and faith healers, including Oral

Roberts. Gordon's group sponsored the first convention of healing evangelists in Dallas, Texas, in 1949.

In the 1960s, Gordon moved to the Dallas neighborhood of Oak Cliff where he conducted seminars on Spirit-filled Christianity. Those seminars led to the creation of a Bible school, which, in turn, gave Gordon the vision for the Christ For The Nations Institute for young people interested in Spirit-filled or charismatic worship. CFNI opened in 1970 with about fifty students. It had grown to nearly 250 when Gordon passed away in 1973 while participating in a Sunday worship service on the stage of the school's new $1 million auditorium.

Upon Gordon's passing, the school's all-male board asked Freda, who was schooled in Pentecostal evangelism at L.I.F.E Bible College, founded by Aimee Semple McPherson, to step into his role and take charge. Known to CFNI students as "Mom Lindsay," Freda grew up in a family of twelve children, all of whom worked in the farm fields of her native Oregon to keep the big family fed. She was eighteen years old when she attended a revival meeting in Portland and met the evangelist Gordon Lindsay at the door as she left. He stopped her there and said, "Freda, I thought this would be your night." She felt the Lord's presence immediately and rushed to the altar.

"I was no big sinner, but I knew I wasn't serving the Lord," she recalls. "That night I felt the Lord speak to me and say, 'Freda, if you follow Me, obey Me, walk faithfully in pureness, you will one day marry this evangelist.'"

She and Gordon married five years later. Shortly after they were married, Freda developed tuberculosis in both lungs. Doctors gave her only eighteen months to live, but she and Gordon prayed and the Lord healed her. It was a miracle, to be certain. Sometimes, though, the symptoms would return when Freda came under stress, so she says, "I learned to pace myself." Apparently she learned to do it very well.

Though she had always been a partner in her husband's work, Freda was at first daunted by the prospect of continuing it upon Gordon's passing. She also was made aware that some believed that a woman shouldn't be allowed to even speak in church. In the 1970s, Freda's role didn't sit well with some who believed women should not be in such a leadership position. "I'd get letters chewing me out, but I'd tell them that it was the men who put me in this position," she remembers.

At first, Freda says, she was all but paralyzed with uncertainty. She wondered how in the world she could continue with the grand vision and mission set forth by her late husband.

Freda's story is amazing because as she surrendered this incredible challenge to God, He began to direct her and show her how to proceed. Even those who had at first doubted her would come to praise Freda as an organizational genius and a masterful fund-raiser. She wiped out much of the school's debt in just a few years while continuing to expand the student population and its campus.

Under her guidance the institute took over nearby apartment buildings and a hotel for student housing and classrooms. She expanded the music program and reached out to create Bible schools and build churches in other nations. Her son, Dennis Lindsay, is now in charge of CFNI, where about one fourth of the students are foreign. The school even has a Spanish-language division for Hispanic students.

Under Freda's leadership, CFNI grew to become much bigger and greater than anyone could have imagined. It has a global reach extending into 120 nations and teaching the Word of God through associated Bible institutes. It also has published 60 million books in eighty-two languages.

CFNI supporters aid in worldwide relief projects, and they have assisted native congregations in building more than 12,000 churches all over the world. CFNI has Associate Bible schools in forty-four areas around the world including Germany, Belarus, Moldova, Romania, Brazil, Japan, and India. More than 30,000 students have been trained at CFNI and empowered by the Spirit to touch others with the same gospel that has transformed their lives. Every year about two hundred international students at CFNI agree to return to their native countries to minister.

Freda is now in her nineties, and when we get together for events, we reflect on her experiences and how they serve as an example of the power of surrender. This humble woman became one of God's great leaders when she asked Him to help her take up the challenge. It was her early surrender that made this school what it is today, and the impact of that decision will continue to make the world a better, godlier place for decades to come. In April 2007, Freda participated in the dedication of the Freda Lindsay World Missions Center that will house the Spanish school, the School of Missions, the School of Youth Ministry, the Youth For The Nations, and Spanish YFN programs, as well as a twenty-four-hour prayer room dedicated to her husband, Gordon.

She says that whenever she completes one of her goals, such as the creation of the world missions center, she prays to the Lord for guidance to find new goals because, as her life illustrates, when you surrender your career—and your life—to God, your prayers can move mountains.

6

Surrender Your Health

etty Baxter was born with severe and crippling birth defects that included curvature of her spine, a damaged nervous system, and more medical problems than one person could seem capable of bearing. "My entire body was crippled up and deformed," she says in a testimony she gave during a church service I was attending.

Betty dwelled in a place with no hope. Her pain was physical as well as emotional. As a child, it took two or three injections of morphine to give her any relief. Her doctor eventually took her off the narcotic drug because it was causing her more harm than good. Her body had gotten so accustomed to it that the pain persisted.

"Oh, how long the nights were as I lay racked with pain. Many times I would twist in the bed struggling for a little relief and feel myself blacking out. Then for hours I would lay unconscious."[1]

Betty was from a Christian family. She'd been taught by her mother that Jesus heals those who believe and have faith in Him. She'd heard the story of

Jesus's birth in the manger, His life and the miracles He performed, His torture and death on the cross, and His resurrection. It was "the best story" she had ever heard, and it inspired her to ask Jesus to help save her from her sins.

At the age of nine, she had a vision: "I saw before me a big door in the shape of a heart. Jesus walked up to that door and listened in. There was no knob or latch on the outside. Then Jesus knocked once and listened, then the second, and the third time He knocked the door flew open; Jesus walked in and I knew I was saved. I felt the great burden of sin roll off of me." It was then that she decided to become an evangelist.

But Betty's journey of surrender had only begun. Her health deteriorated, and two years later, she was blind, deaf, and mute. Paralyzed, her body was twisted and clenched. Her kidneys were shutting down, and doctors said she was on the verge of death. "It seemed I was caught; some awful power was trying to destroy me."

She prayed. Her family prayed. She began to hear Jesus speaking to her softly, telling her that He loved her. She held on to her faith, telling Jesus she was ready for His Father's kingdom: *Please come and take me to that place called heaven.*

She slipped into "darkness" and saw a long, narrow valley—the valley of death. Prepared to die, she decided to reject her fears. "To get to Jesus I will have to walk it" she told herself. She had taken just a few steps when the dark valley was filled with light. She felt a strong hand grasp hers. "He took my hand and held it tightly, and I went on through the valley." Her fear evaporated as her surrender was complete. "I was happy, for now I was going home."

She walked on, recalling that her mother had told her that in heaven she would have a body free of deformities and pain. Betty heard beautiful music as she walked. She came to a wide river and saw a beautiful place of green grass and bright flowers on the other side. "I saw the river of life winding its way through the city of God."

Before she could cross, Jesus spoke to her. "Go back and fulfill the call I gave you when you were nine years old. Go back, for you are going to have healing in the fall." That August Jesus came to heal Betty, and she was completely made whole. Betty saw a vision of Jesus as He walked into the room where she was sitting. She looked into His face, and she said she saw the kindest eyes she had ever seen. He reached down to touch her, and her crippled body was instantly healed, and for the first time she was able to take a full breath. Betty would go on to fulfill her purpose on the earth as she got involved in missions and preached the gospel to all who would listen. Each time Betty would share her miracle story, people would be inspired and people would be healed.

Betty draws powerful lessons from her experiences. I once heard her tell an audience about speaking with a young man who'd been paralyzed from the waist down in a motorcycle accident. He came to four or five of her appearances, and at each he asked her to pray for his recovery. Finally, she asked him, "If God were to heal you, would you be willing to do what He wanted you to do and to be what He wanted you to be?"

The paralyzed man said he would not be willing to do that because "He might ask me to do something I don't want to do."

As she recounted the man's response, Betty, who had experienced a medical miracle because of her own faith, looked up at the audience and offered this simple but powerful lesson: "When you have tried everything else, why don't you try surrender?"

Kristie's story

My sister Kristie and I were always close as children, and we are doubly close as adults because we married brothers. She is married to Marcus's brother Gary, who is also a minister, at Northpointe Church in Macon,

Georgia. They have two children, Chase and Krista, who are four years apart. It was shortly after she gave birth to their daughter that my sister, who was then just twenty-five years old, experienced headaches and blurred vision in her left eye.

"I had ignored the same symptoms during my pregnancy," she says. "Then, during my six and a half weeks of leave from my nursing job, I noticed I was having trouble lifting Krista. Still, it wasn't until I went back to working at the hospital as a registered nurse, working twelve-hour shifts in the labor and delivery rooms, that my health problems became even more noticeable."

Kristie was working the night shift when she found she was having trouble reading a patient's chart. She thought maybe her eyes were just tired, but when she looked up at a wall clock she realized that the vision in her left eye was dimmed. The next morning she spoke to a doctor about her dimmed vision. He suggested she see an eye-doctor friend of his that day. He picked up the phone and made the appointment himself, which Kristie took as an indication of his concern.

"I was concerned too because of the headaches, so I went to the eye doctor, who immediately said I should see a neurologist," she says. He, too, made the appointment right then and there. "I told him I had a newborn and a four-year-old and I had just worked twelve hours in the labor and delivery room, but he insisted that I go right away, so my concern escalated."

Fears Realized

Kristie was frightened. She called and told me what was going on. It particularly troubled her because she had been caring for a patient whose vision problems and headaches proved to be symptoms of a brain tumor. She knew the doctors suspected something serious was going on but they were trying to protect her. Her mind was running wild with potential diagnoses.

The neurologist ordered an MRI for that day, but the staff couldn't do it until the next day. Kristie went home and fretted all night. Her physicians had all seemed so concerned, and she was worried she might be dying. She prayed all night and prayed while enclosed in the MRI scanning unit the next morning. It's a little scary being enclosed and unable to move in the scanner, and it's very noisy too. Kristie says she calmed herself by "singing worship songs in my head."

Her fears grew when the radiologist examined the images from her MRI and ordered up another one immediately. This time he had a dye injected into her system so he could see more on the image. After the second MRI, Kristie was told to call the radiologist's office in two days. But before she could do that, the office called Kristie and told her to come in for a meeting—and to bring her husband.

"That was the first time I really broke down," Kristie says. "I was thinking all kinds of things."

She and Gary went the next day, and the physician told her that the MRI and the symptoms were indicative of multiple sclerosis (MS), which is an autoimmune disease. It affects the central nervous system that includes the brain, spinal cord, and optic nerves. On Kristie's MRI, the radiologist had seen what appeared to be deterioration of the fatty tissue or myelin that protects the nerve fibers of the central nervous system and helps them conduct electrical impulses.

When the myelin is lost, it leaves scar tissue called sclerosis. The loss of myelin interferes with the nervous system and produces the various symptoms of MS. Myelin not only protects nerve fibers, it also helps them do their jobs. When myelin or the nerve fiber is destroyed or damaged, the ability of the nerves to conduct electrical impulses to and from the brain is disrupted, producing the wide variety of symptoms associated with MS: vision problems, lack of energy, slurred speech, tremors, and balance problems. It is also not unusual for symptoms to come and go, but sometimes they never cease and only worsen.

In Kristie's case the doctors said the gradual dimming and eventual loss of vision in her left eye, arm weakness, and headaches—along with the MRI results—appeared to make it a "pretty sure thing" that she had MS.

Fears Inflated

Kristie was raised in a Christian home. She and her husband were pastoring a church where she was also the worship leader. She knew that God was present in times of trouble. But in her fear and growing sense of despair, Kristie—my bubbly, joyful, and loving little sister—lost her way. It can happen even to someone of such deep faith. In fact, the Enemy will target true believers in hopes of turning them away from God. That makes Kristie's story all the more important as a lesson to us all.

"The Lord was there, but my problem was that I tried to deal with this challenge on my own strength instead of leaning on my husband and the Word of God," Kristie recalls. "I did not have the realization that God was in control and would lead me through it."

When her family members and other loved ones reached out to Kristie, she insisted that she was doing fine and that God was with her every step of the way. We all thought that she had a good handle on it—as good as might be expected.

But, as it turned out, we were wrong.

"I knew the right things to say, but I didn't believe it in my heart," Kristie admits. "The Enemy was working on my mind, and I began to slip into depression and lose control of my thoughts and actions." Depression set in. Kristie struggled to hide her dark moods and thoughts from us as it slowly ate away at her, destroying her peace of mind and disrupting the faith of a good Christian woman. The battle in her mind became far worse than the symptoms of the disease in her body.

Depression is an insidious disorder. Often it settles in slowly, like a fog moving over you so that at first you don't notice it. You may just feel "a little down" and then, before you have time to react, you are swept in a downward spiral of emotional and mental darkness that can lead to dangerous physical consequences.

"The Enemy began to torment my mind, little by little," says Kristie. "I would see television commercials or roadside billboards about MS, and they would trigger even more depression. I tried to pray, but I'd end up wallowing in despair. I'd hear the Enemy saying things like: 'You won't be able to take care of your own children. You can no longer be a mother to them. You will become dead weight to your husband.'"

The Enemy of her soul was preying on her vulnerability, trying to destroy my sweet sister, and she was hiding it from me and everyone else who loved her. Kristie says, "I became one person in public and another when I was alone." She fed and bathed and took care of her children, going through the motions of motherhood, but slowly she withdrew emotionally from them and her husband.

"I became selfish in my depression," she says. "It was all about me and what was happening to me. I felt worthless and, as a result, I came to the conclusion that it was best if I just stopped living. One night I found myself driving our family van as if I'd awakened from a dream. The Enemy's voice was in my ear: 'You can end it now and be done with this pain. Gary will be fine with the kids. Your life insurance will take care of them for the rest of their lives. It's better to go fast than to die slowly in front of them, dragging them down with you.'

"I remember pressing the accelerator as the van approached a bridge. I don't know how fast I was going, but it was faster than I'd ever driven. I had the thought of turning into the path of an oncoming car so that it would hit the van and knock it off the bridge," Kristie remembers. "Then, just as that instantaneous urge struck me, I glanced into the rearview mirror and realized that both kids were in their car seats in the back seat. Yet the Enemy said: 'End your pain. They shouldn't have to suffer.'"

Praise God, Kristie didn't obey the voice.

"The van must have been going about ninety miles per hour at that point, and I don't know how it happened, but somehow God slowed it down," Kristie says. "We came to the bottom of a hill, and it just slowed down. I began to cry and again I looked in the mirror and saw my babies— and I realized that the Enemy was out to destroy me and my children. I couldn't believe that I'd come so close to doing it. In horror I realized that I'd been preparing to kill another person too, the driver of the oncoming car. I'd become some other person."

Her children had slept through the whole thing, and Kristie, horrified at what had occurred, did not tell Gary. The more she thought about it, the more horrified she became. For the first time, she was able to step back and study her own frightening deterioration—from the family's eternal optimist into a deeply depressed and suicidal person who had put her children and a complete stranger at risk. Flashes of the van on the bridge kept coming back to her over the next few days. She withdrew even more, afraid of her own thoughts, until one night she broke down as she slept on the couch, away from her husband in the bedroom.

She was crying so hard she was afraid she'd awaken Gary and the children, so she went into the bathroom and ran water in the tub. "I was crying like I had never cried before," she says. Gary woke up, knocked on the door, and asked what was wrong. Kristie calmed herself then and got dressed. They sat down together, and she told him that she had nearly killed herself and Chase and Krista in the van.

"I need you to know and I need you to forgive me," she told her husband.

Gary was stunned, but he comforted her. "The Enemy cannot have you. We're going to break his hold right now," he said.

He prayed over her, calling on the Lord with powerful prayers, and Kristie felt the release of the Enemy's hold on her. The suicidal thoughts were gone, but the depression lingered still. Confessing to Gary was just the first step. Over the next few days, they prayed together and individually, asking the Lord's forgiveness.

Finally, Kristie surrendered her illness to His care. She says, "The Lord began to reveal the pathway to my healing."

With Gary there to support her and to stand in faith with her, they started down the path by reading healing Scriptures. The Lord spoke to Gary and told him they had to build hope and faith because Kristie was still in the throes of depression. Together they looked up healing Scriptures and put them on index cards. Kristie then placed the cards all over the house and around her workplace, taping them to mirrors and the refrigerator, on her work locker and clipboards, and on the visor of the van.

"The people at work thought I was nuts because I didn't tell them what had happened. I didn't tell anyone but Gary for more than a year," she remembers. "I was so ashamed and mortified."

Fears Relieved

We tend to seek miracles and instant healing, but the truth is that even when you surrender your illness to the Lord, most of the time you don't get a miracle overnight. God works on His own schedule, for His own purposes. Kristie's was a progressive healing, but it was no less a miracle.

As her depression and shame lifted slowly, over the course of about a year and a half, it dawned on Kristie that her headaches, arm weakness, and vision problems were gone too.

"As I walked in faith on the Path of Surrender, I drew closer and closer to God the healer, and it was only then that I realized I was not experiencing the symptoms," she says.

She had not even noticed it when the Enemy had a hold on her, but once she was free, Kristie realized that the symptoms associated with MS had disappeared. Gary told her that while God has the power to heal instantly, often He wants us to go through a progression so that we appreciate and understand the healing that has occurred.

Since MS symptoms are known to come and go, Kristie continued treatment and even signed up for a lottery to get an experimental medication. She was one of the few to be chosen in the lottery for the drug, which was very expensive, around $10,000 a month.

Because her symptoms had disappeared, Kristie had allowed herself to have hope again. She did not want to take the medicine unless the Lord directed her to do it. They decided to see a Macon neurologist who specialized in MS to see if he thought she should take the costly experimental medication.

"Gary and I were having lunch at Wendy's just before my appointment with the specialist, and I just broke down crying, telling him that if the MS symptoms returned, I couldn't handle it," Kristie recalls.

During her examination that day, the neurologist seemed confused as he examined her left eye. "I'd told him that I had been blind for months in that eye, but he said he couldn't find any indication that there was anything wrong with it," Kristie says. "He asked if I was certain that it was my left eye that had the problem."

After a complete physical exam, the neurologist stunned my sister and her husband, telling them he could find no evidence of MS.

God loves us all in equal measure, and His Word is so powerful. Jesus said that He will never leave us nor forsake us no matter what we are going through. But we must have faith. We must acknowledge His presence in our lives and surrender to the Lord's will.

Kristie knew that, but she so quickly became overwhelmed that she lost her way. "If I had simply had faith in the Father and used what He had given me in a wonderful, godly husband, I would not have spiraled into suicide and wanted to kill myself," she says now. She realizes now that her husband, Gary, was there to help her and encourage her. But then, instead of going to him, she retreated inside herself. When she finally realized that God could use her husband to encourage her and stand with her as the head of their home, she was able to join her faith with the faith of her godly husband, and together they were able to weather the storm that had blown into their lives.

Salvation is the greatest gift the Lord can give us. He restored Kristie's joy in life and gave her back her marriage and health. She found peace, and her body was healed and restored through her surrender to the Lord's will.

God knows every tear you have cried, every ache and pain, every doubt, every hurt. He is a healing Father, and we need to trust in Him as Kristie came to do, once again. It is never too late. There is always hope.

Pam's Story

Pam Tebow, who has served as a missionary in the Philippines with her husband in the Bob Tebow Evangelistic Association, understands the power of daily surrender. In an interview, she told a Gainesville, Florida, newspaper reporter that they taught their own five children "that in everything you give thanks to the Lord. There's something supernatural that takes place when you trade your anxieties for God's peace."[2]

Pam noted that she surrendered to God's will in 1985 while serving in the Philippines when she contracted amebic dysentery and took strong medications. Shortly after that she found out she was pregnant. Doctors told her that the fetus had been irreversibly damaged by the drugs, and they advised her to have an abortion. She refused, surrendering her health to the Lord's will in the belief that He would guide this child. She spent the last two months of her pregnancy on bed rest, and then on August 14, 1987, she gave birth to a healthy baby boy.

Twenty years later, Pam and Bob Tebow stood on a stage in New York City with that child, their son Timmy, as he thanked Jesus Christ, "my Lord and Savior," after becoming the youngest person ever to win the Heisman Trophy, awarded to the person considered to be the best college football player in the country. The record-breaking University of Florida sophomore quarterback accounted for fifty-one touchdowns in his first season as a starter, throwing twenty-nine touchdown passes and running for another twenty-two during the regular season.

Debbie's Story

If there was ever someone who serves as an example that people of faith should never say never, it was Debbie Mason. Her life is an absolute testimony to the power of surrendering your health to God's will.

Debbie and her husband, Bob, were the driving forces and founders of Missions International-World Expeditions. They had served in missions in over sixty countries. When they weren't trekking around the world, they shared their vision for missions, praise and worship, and development of local church leadership. This dynamic and godly couple had been married more than twenty-seven years and they had two children, Daniella Carina and Christian Robert.

Debbie, a beautiful singer who grew up in a missionary family, felt strongly that the Bible is God's Word and those words come to pass if we dare to believe. Psalm 34:19 tells us that "many are the afflictions of the righteous, but the LORD delivers him out of them all."

We face many challenges in our Christian lives, but Debbie held that our Redeemer and Savior wants to prove that He can do great miracles. "So believe in Him, and don't give up," she said.

Debbie believed and she never gave up, not even when she was struck a cruel, tortuous, and disfiguring blow. This devout woman of God was laid low at the age of thirty-four by cancer of the tongue that spread into the bone of her jaw. This rare and fast-spreading form of cancer usually afflicts only elderly individuals who've been smokers and heavy drinkers. Debbie had never done either.

Initially, doctors told Debbie that the cancer might kill her, and if it didn't she would certainly never be able to sing again. They had to remove a third of her tongue and a large section of her jaw in a series of operations. Debbie feared that her days of ministering were over, that her husband would never again find her attractive, and that she would never again know the joy of singing God's praises.

Those are the sort of thoughts that the Enemy plants in the minds of the faithful—like my sister and my friend Debbie—when they are faced with tremendous health challenges. You, too, can expect such thoughts to attack you, but know that you and the Lord are up to the challenge. "The

Devil spoke to me every morning. It was basically the same thing: 'You are going to die anyway so you might as well give up now. Everybody who looks at you thinks you are going to die.' "

For her first operation, the doctors told Debbie that they would remove a third of her tongue and the lymph nodes in her mouth. Her husband asked them to give God time to work: "We believe in miracles," Bob told them.

The doctors agreed to give her two weeks. Debbie used the time to walk the Path of Surrender, fasting and praying as she went—with the understanding that if nothing changed in her condition, they would proceed.

During this time, Bob and Debbie went to see a dear friend who was in ministry. "He prayed the prayer of faith and said something strange that I didn't expect," said Debbie. "He said the Lord wanted us to do everything the doctors told us to do. I thought that was unusual because I came from a family that preached faith healing. We never went to doctors. So it was a step of faith for me to do that."

Debbie and Bob sought a second medical opinion. This physician told her that she had a 40 to 60 percent chance of living. "My husband piped up again and said, 'But she is a singer...' and I'm thinking, 'This doctor is telling me I'm going to die and you are worried about my singing?'

"Then the doctor said, 'You can forget about singing. You will never sing again.' But Bob said the Holy Spirit came just then and told him that I would sing again and when I sang that people would be healed, delivered, and set free."

All of this had Debbie very upset. "I was so petrified I never thought to ask the doctor whether he meant I had a 40 percent chance to live or a 60 percent chance to live."

Miraculous Healing

Debbie went ahead with the operation, in which the surgeons took out a third of her tongue and portions of the left side of her face because of the cancer. Six months later, they had to go back in because they found two tumors under her teeth in her jaw. She then had twelve hours of reconstructive surgery. Just three days after that, they found more cancer in her jaw, so they had to go back in and remove all of her jaw. Doctors then put a titanium plate where her jaw had been.

Just before one of Debbie's many surgeries, a friend had a vision that comforted her and her loved ones, which she recounted in her book *He Held My Hand.* "Just as I was going in for my fourteen-hour jaw surgery, Joyce, a Baptist lady I'd met during this process, had a dream in which she saw me on an operating-room table with six doctors around me. At the head of the bed was Jesus and He was holding my hand."

Joyce woke up from the dream so excited that she called Bob at the hospital and told him, "Jesus is on the fourth floor, holding your wife's hand." She then described what she'd dreamed, including the six doctors. Bob, of course, was thrilled by what Joyce was telling him, and he mentioned it to the nurse in charge of the surgery floor. She told him that there were only supposed to be three doctors involved in Debbie's surgery, but that at the last minute, three more had offered to assist.

"When Bob heard that, he got really excited," Debbie said. "When I heard all this, it really got me, too, because the night before the surgery, I'd reached for my Bible and it had just opened up to Isaiah 41:13, which says: "For I, the LORD your God, will hold your right hand, saying to you, 'Fear not, I will help you.'"

Debbie did find strength so that even with all of that pain and suffering and stress, she took joy in the fact that doctors were able to hide the plate inside her face so that her two-year-old daughter would not be afraid to look at her.

"It took them another year and a half to reconstruct my jaw and face, putting me back together like Humpty Dumpty," she said. "I think they did pretty good considering I lost so much of my face and several teeth too. I went two years without teeth before they gave me new ones, and I found that the Lord had a Scripture for that too. In Isaiah 41:15, he says: "Behold, I will make you into a new threshing sledge with sharp teeth; you shall thresh the mountains and beat them small, and make the hills like chaff."

Debbie endured years of surgery and therapy and defied all medical expectations. She not only recovered, but she and Bob had another child, Christian Robert, after all of her surgeries.

Even more miraculous is the fact that despite the projections of all of her doctors, Debbie reclaimed her singing voice. Technically, she should not have been able to sing a note because of the surgeries to her tongue and jaw, but Debbie sang beautifully on my show and around the world in recent years. She sings and the Spirit of the Lord touches people in special ways. Her life serves as a testimony of the power of surrender for everyone facing health challenges. As she said in her own prayers, "Father God, we thank You that Your presence is so real and no obstacle is too difficult for You. You are a great God who hears and answers every prayer."

Debbie was diagnosed with a deadly cancer over twenty-one years ago. It would have killed the average person, but Debbie was anything but average. She was one of the most godly human beings I have ever met. She touched the lives of everyone she met, and she was an incredible light of God's love to the world.

Miraculously Home

Debbie was cancer-free for seventeen years. She was able to defeat cancer the first go round with her faith in God and belief in His Word. However, in 2007 she was afflicted with a new cancer. We were all concerned about the new battle that would ensue, knowing that our precious friend had already been through so much.

I hadn't seen Debbie for several weeks, and as I was driving home one night, I felt the Lord impress me to stop by and see her. I'm not one to drop in unannounced, but with a strong sense that I needed to do so, I made my way to Bob and Debbie's house. I got to see my friend and visit for a few minutes and we prayed together. I had no idea it would be the last time I would see her.

A few weeks later, in December 2007, I learned that Debbie had gone on to meet the Lord. Her husband, Bob, told me that she was fully prepared to fight the second battle with cancer, but instead she had peacefully gone to sleep one afternoon and joined the Lord. Bob told me that cancer did not take our beloved Debbie.

I attended the funeral of Debbie Mason, and Bob asked me to say a few words about my friend. I read from 1 Corinthians 13:4–7: "Love suffers long and is kind; love does not envy;…love…does not seek its own, is not provoked, thinks no evil; does not rejoice in iniquity, but rejoices in the truth; bears all things, believes all things, hopes all things, endures all things." These verses describe my friend Debbie Mason. I believe that even now she's singing with the heavenly chorus and making preparations for those of us who will one day meet with her in eternity.

Our Story

We are God's creations, made in the image of a loving and caring Father. Through Him, we experience love, compassion, peace, and hope. We all have the desire and the ability to pursue life to its fullest, to live and experience relationships, to find purpose and meaning, to be needed and feel wanted. Yet when we experience serious health challenges, the ability and even the desire to pursue and experience life can be severely compromised.

It is so important that we take care of this earthly vessel that God has given us by eating wisely and exercising regularly. He tells us in 2 Corinthians 4:7: "We have this treasure in earthen vessels, that the excellence of the power may be of God and not of us." God even lays out the menu in the Levitical diet, which is what kosher Jews follow for healthy living.

Of course, even those who get plenty of sleep, eat wisely, and exercise regularly can get sick. When you have done all you can do to protect the vessel and your health is still challenged, you must walk the Path of Surrender.

Years ago a pastor's wife we know was diagnosed with melanoma cancer on her leg. By the time the doctors caught it, the prognosis was not good. She told me that she had everyone praying for her but nothing had changed.

"Joni, I looked at that melanoma and said: 'Yes, I have to acknowledge that this is cancer, and I have to acknowledge that this could kill me, but I *only* acknowledge it, knowing that God is greater than this melanoma.'" This woman of faith was completely healed, and she lives today as a testimony to God's healing power.

The Lord created us and He can show us the path to healing of all kinds. Cancer, disease, a broken-down body, or any other serious health challenge can exhaust your spirit as well as your physical energies. You may come to feel that your life has lost purpose or that you are no longer useful or needed. Depression can darken your dreams and desires. In your pain, grief, and exhaustion, you may well feel that you are alone and unloved.

But you are not. Even in the most challenging of times, you can experience hope. During such dark times, the smallest thing you can do becomes the most you can do: Pray to the Lord. Surrender your health to God's plan. Express your faith in His healing power and His wisdom. Do not give up.

7

Surrender Your
Friendships

Kathy had been my best friend all through high school. She was special because when my family had built a new home and moved out into the country, I began attending a new high school, and it was difficult for me to start all over with friends in a new school setting. On my first day, Kathy was in my class, and everyone was talking about the "new girl," who happened to be me. Kathy reached out to me and took me under her wing. She was a true friend and really made me feel welcome. I'll never forget her kindness to me that day, and that would be the start of our friendship.

In an all too typical mean-girls move, another girl came into the picture and befriended me. The only problem was she didn't really want me to be Kathy's best friend. She tried to turn me against Kathy by saying hurtful things about her and making fun of her. Once she wrote me a note about Kathy and put it in the hood of my jacket, trying to be sneaky so Kathy wouldn't see it. I reached around to get the note and Kathy saw me. She asked what the note was about, but I didn't want to tell her. I knew it would hurt her to see it, but I think she knew we were talking about her behind her back.

I tried to figure out a way to be friends with both of them, but it simply wasn't working. I let it go for a while but finally told Kathy what this girl was saying. I felt so much better for telling her the truth, but in retaliation, the mean girl then made me the target, trying to turn Kathy and anyone else she could convince against me. It didn't matter what I did from that point on, the mean girl never forgave me for telling Kathy, and she made it a point to make my life miserable no matter how hard I tried to reconcile everyone.

I spent many hours wrestling with the "ifs" and "whys" of how this or that had happened in my high school social circle. I'd get stressed out when there was friction between friends because I wanted everyone to get along. But I had to stand by Kathy and face the wrath of the mean girl, even though Kathy did not understand the price I paid for my loyalty. I doubt if Kathy ever really knew how spiteful this other girl was, but eventually I got over it and concentrated on other friends as well as my friendship with Kathy. I don't regret the decision I made to be honest.

Friendship carries a lot of meaning for me. I have always cherished my friends, and I have always tried to be a good friend. The ever-shifting, self-serving, and often false friendships of early high school bothered me greatly because I invested and trusted so much in these relationships.

It is easy to dismiss teen drama as childish when you aren't caught up in it, but emotions are powerful at that age. Teens are flooded with hormones.

Their brains are rewiring themselves, so it doesn't take much to throw them off balance. I sympathize with my own teenage children because I remember how it was. Back then I believed that my high school friends would be close for the rest of my life.

Betrayal

The friendships that I cared about so much in high school pale in comparison to the much deeper and more mature relationships that come with adulthood. The betrayal of a friendship in adulthood can be a devastating experience. It is one of the deepest hurts I've felt.

In one particularly hurtful case, I totally misread a person who portrayed herself as a friend. This person, out of selfishness, betrayed our friendship and left me feeling wounded and deeply disappointed. She became like part of my family, helping with my kids, walking and exercising with me, and visiting my home often. She presented herself as a loyal and faithful friend, and I trusted her and embraced her. Slowly I began to see that she wanted to interact with my friends, be close to my kids and family, and move into the circle of influence given to her with my friendship—and she seemed to want it all more than friendship itself. Trusting as I was, I tried to help her through some difficult circumstances in her life and tried to be a true friend. But she repeatedly broke one of the Ten Commandments: "Thou shalt not covet" (KJV).

It would serve no purpose to detail the depth of her betrayal here. But what is important is how her actions affected me and how I pressed through this difficult friendship. When I discovered that this supposed friend had engaged in a very thorough campaign of betrayal, I was floored with utter shock and dismay. It was debilitating to contemplate the lengths she had gone to in her efforts. She had deceived me so thoroughly that for a time I was in denial that I could have been so blind to her scheme.

Only God knows someone's heart, but it is my guess that there was deceit in this woman's heart long before she met me. I wouldn't even try to offer an excuse or judge her motivation. Perhaps there had been disappointing situations in her life that left her wounded and incapable of trustworthiness. I would like to believe that something in her past was responsible for her actions. We cannot judge others. We just don't know what they have been through. All we can do is forgive and move on. I too eventually had to surrender my wounds to God. If we harbor bitterness or anger or despair, those emotions can eat away at our mental, physical, and spiritual well-being.

To Keep or Not to Keep

Offering up my pain to God in total surrender was almost impossible for me. It was beyond my ability to understand, but I believed that, somehow, God would see me through. I had to visualize myself literally handing all of the hurt over to God. It helps me to use visualization when I undertake an act of surrender. I see myself as a little child coming before His throne and handing Him all this emotional "junk."

When I imagine that scene of handing over my burden to God, I am overcome with feelings. I feel His compassion. His love. His kindness. His mercy. Often in my surrender scenarios, God tells me I must forgive and I tell Him I cannot. It is too hurtful, I say. He tells me He will help me. And though it is hard to believe or comprehend, I must, as a child of God, believe my Father and allow Him to walk me, hand in hand, through the process of forgiveness and healing.

In some cases God may choose to heal a broken friendship or relationship. But it is important to understand that in other instances, He may decide to let the bonds wither and die. It may be that God sees a relationship as toxic for one or both parties, so He intervenes. It is in your best interest to surrender to God's decision and let it stand. You may be reading this and thinking of a particular friendship that is toxic and should be brought to an end. I want to encourage you to surrender this relationship to the Lord and ask Him to reveal the truth to you so that you can make a wise decision. You may not like what the Lord shows you—whether to drop the relationship or keep it—but I guarantee you that His plan is good. He may be guiding you to a more meaningful and healthier relationship, or He may be guiding you to a new level in the current relationship. Right now it may be hard to believe that either scenario could be possible, but that's okay; all you have to believe is that God knows what He is doing.

Blessing After Betrayal

I have found that when we surrender the most difficult of circumstances, we often receive a blessing on the other side of the trial—something that would not have been realized unless we were willing to give up control and allow God to do what He needs to do in our lives.

My producer, Karen Thompson, has shared with me her experiences with two former friends whom she believes God decided to let loose from her. In both cases it was difficult to let go, but Karen ultimately surrendered and committed herself to letting Him show her the way.

"The Lord needed to take me to another level, so I had to surrender those friendships," she says. "It was really hard but it had to be done."

One of the friends was a boss who had been like a brother to Karen. She was adopted as a child, so she has a special regard for friendships of this kind. She doesn't form them easily or give up on them easily either. She had worked with him early in her career and then followed him after he took a job elsewhere because she had such a high regard for him. It was a very trusting relationship that grew over the years to include their spouses and children. They went on vacations together and shared in family events and celebrations.

But then things went sour. They had a falling out. He left the company under a cloud. At first she was angry. She wondered why the Lord would want her to lose a relationship that had been so supportive and fulfilling. She had looked up to her friend and thought he had creative powers that were beyond her grasp.

But once she surrendered the friendship to the Lord, the Father revealed to Karen that she had been living in her friend's shadow. He cast such a wide shadow that it kept her from developing and bringing her own talents to light. "I always said that he was the creative one and I just gave legs to his ideas," Karen says. But now she found that her own creative strengths expanded far beyond what she'd ever thought possible. "I never thought I could be an idea person, but once I surrendered the relationship, the Lord showed me it was in my brain and helped me let go of my insecurities."

As sometimes happens, this former friend eventually tried to get back into her life. But by that time, Karen had moved on. She bloomed into an amazing creative producer and learned from the past friendship that she could be healthier removed from a controlling friend that distracted her from God's plan and purpose for her life.

Later Karen went through a similar situation with a close friend who made it clear that she no longer wished to continue their friendship. Again she felt hurt and betrayed, but this time she was stronger because of her previous experience in surrendering a friendship to the Lord. And this time, she also drew strength from advice she heard from T. D. Jakes. Bishop

Jakes said that if people decide they want to walk out of your life, let them. Then the Lord sent her even more encouragement when Joyce Meyer appeared on my show. Joyce noted that sometimes the Lord will move people out of your life so He can move you where He wants you to be.

"I've learned to leave all of my friendships up to the Lord," Karen now says, "because He has shown me that He can take me to new levels of accomplishment in my life and in my friendships."

The Ultimate Betrayal

When I find it difficult to surrender a friendship or relationship that has gone sour, I reflect on Jesus and the many times He was betrayed by those He loved. I wonder how Jesus must have felt when Judas, one of His beloved twelve disciples, betrayed Him in the garden. I cannot imagine the pain Jesus experienced when one that He trusted and loved sold Him out for thirty pieces of silver. How did Jesus feel when another beloved disciple, Peter, denied Him?

When we endure a betrayal by a friend or loved one, we need to remember that there is One who experienced far worse betrayals, and yet He forgave. I encourage you to remember what Jesus endured from His select group of friends. The Bible says he is "touched with the feeling of our infirmities" (Hebrews 4:15, KJV). Jesus knows every pain and hurt you will ever experience. He can help you deal with your pain, help you surrender it to the Father, just as He did.

As you surrender the pain of your betrayal to Him, He will heal you and He will stand by His promise of never leaving you nor forsaking you (see Deuteronomy 31:6) I can absolutely rest in the assurance of God's promise to me that even though people and circumstances of life may fail me, He will not (see 2 Thessalonians 3:3).

True Friends

It is one thing to surrender a friendship that has hurt you, but how do you surrender a true friendship?

First of all, to surrender this blessed gift to God, we have to be able to recognize what a true friendship is. Along with unwavering faith in Jesus Christ, there are four primary virtues I look for in my closest relationships:

1. *Trustworthiness.* We can confide in each other, knowing that we will keep each other's confidence. The best friendships are low maintenance because they are so high in trust.

2. *Loyalty.* We stand by each other in good times and in bad times. True friends do not betray; they may, however, hurt. Proverbs 27:6 says that a friend will wound you with the truth. Friends who are trustworthy speak the loving truth even if it hurts. A true friend cares more about the truth than trying to say what you want to hear. As you surrender friendships to the Lord, He can show you clearly who to trust and who to be careful of. True friendships are built upon mutual respect and understanding.

3. *Dependability.* We know that we can always count on each other. Such friendships endure. They don't fall apart, even when other relationships and responsibilities reduce the time you can spend together. True friends know their relationship will endure even when they are apart.

4. *Companionship.* We can laugh together, cry together, and pray together without self-consciousness. True friends don't put demands on the friendship or on each other—or place each other in uncomfortable positions. You know that a friend-ship is healthy and balanced when you are never made to feel stressed out or guilty for failing to live up to unreasonable expectations. Too many friendships fail because one or both

parties have the "if" factor, as in "If you were really my friend, you would…" True friends serve each other by looking out for the other's best interests.

Second, to surrender this blessed gift to God, we have to know when to hold on to a friendship and when to release it or let it go. There will be times when it is clear that a friendship is worth saving, and even though there are difficult times, we walk in love, forgive, and work through the issues of life.

There are also those times when it will be clear to us that certain friendships are not healthy and we should end them. I was reading a message by Brian Houston, pastor of Hillsong Church in Sydney, Australia, and he mentioned the questions that we must ask ourselves when deciding about friendships:

- Is it hurting my relationship with God?
- Is it distracting me from my call and purpose?
- Is it destructive to the work of the Lord?
- Is it helpful to my marriage and family?[1]

It's pretty obvious that with the first three questions, if the answer is yes, that those kinds of friendships aren't good. Your relationship with God comes first, and you don't need a friendship that's distracting you from your call and purpose. If a friendship is hurting the work of the Lord, then you need to stay away from that friendship. If the answer to the last question is no, then you need to end this friendship immediately. God instituted the family and refers to us as his children. Any friendship that takes away from the family is not a godly friendship.

My Friends

Friendships that are true bless me and lift my spirits. I never take friendships like this for granted. They enrich my life, and just thinking about them elevates my mood.

Besides Marcus, who happens to be my very best friend, I have several really close friends—women who warm my heart when I think of them: my precious mother; my sister, Kristie; Lynn; Cindy; Rhonda; and Sam. I'm blessed to have many special friends, but most of us have only a few very close friends whom we can always count on.

I have several lifelong friendships, and one of the most blessed is my friendship with my only sister, Kristie. Our bonds go beyond family loyalty and sisterhood. I also count my two sisters-in-law, Cathy and Tricia, as loyal friends, as well as my sweet mother-in-law, Réne.

I also am truly blessed to have a long and deep friendship with Lynn Blair, whom I met when I was eighteen. We worked together in the offices of J. E. Sirrine Company, the engineering firm where I was hired soon after high school. We bonded at a time when our futures were uncertain. Neither of us had much in the way of material things. We were there for each other through challenging times. We shared tears as well as laughter. She walked with me in those early days through good times and bad times, and she always loved me unconditionally.

Before I met Marcus, Lynn and I often would go on vacation trips together, usually to the beach because we share a love of the ocean—and good food. Of course, back then we were both so skinny, we could eat whatever we wanted. And, boy, did we eat! We also cracked each other up by teasing each other and laughing at our own foibles. (I do a very good Lynn imitation.) At the same time, we enjoy discussing more serious matters of faith and family. We have always been committed to God and eager to follow His plan for our lives.

Lynn was a part of my life when I met Marcus. She was there to see the engagement ring and to share my joy. True friends are happy for each other. They believe that there is enough happiness and joy to go around, so they are glad to see good things happen for the other person. And they want to share in the happiness. Lynn was one of my bridesmaids. She also was one of my biggest supporters when God called me away from her side and we no longer lived in the same town, or even the same state. When I told her that we were moving away, she shared that she would miss me, but she encouraged me to follow God's plan.

Our friendship, trust, and mutual affection has continued unabated for twenty-eight years. Lynn is such a good friend and such an important part of my life that my staff recently flew her to Texas to surprise me for my birthday. It was fitting because a lasting and trusting friendship is one of the greatest gifts the Lord can bestow upon us. I would trust Lynn with my life. She has all of the virtues and qualities I look for in a friend, and even though we live in different states and at times go long periods without seeing one another, we always pick up right where we left off at our last meeting.

One of the things that I love about our friendship is that we never argue or get mad at each other. Our personalities have always seemed perfectly matched. Lynn is so easygoing and kind natured, she makes me feel like a better person because of our friendship—and that is a wonderful thing. She is unselfish and so kind; I will be forever grateful for her love and support.

Just recently Lynn invited us to her home church in South Carolina. I went with the Daystar Singers, and we ministered there on a Sunday morning. It was a great experience to have my friend sitting in the front row beaming at me, sharing God's blessings and feeling His grace. It was a moment I will never forget as I reflect over our years of friendship.

Your Very Best Friend

Marcus preaches a sermon called "Life's Greatest Companion" that is one of my favorites—and not just because he is my husband! In it, he quotes Proverbs 18:24, "A man who has friends must himself be friendly, but there is a friend who sticks closer than a brother."

That friend is Jesus, of course. He is life's greatest companion. You can trust Him. He loves you unconditionally. He will never leave you.

God blesses us with friendships and strong relationships, especially those that last a lifetime. It's important to pick friends who share your belief system and to welcome relationships that are based on mutual trust and affection rather than self-interest. This is one of the many lessons from the Bible's parable of the prodigal son. This son went to his father and asked for his inheritance. When he got it, he left home, breaking his father's heart. "And not many days after, the younger son gathered all together, journeyed to a far country, and there wasted his possessions with prodigal living" (Luke 15:13).

The wasteful son had many friends while the money lasted, and everyone enjoyed the party as they spent his inheritance, but when the money ran out so did those so-called friends. The son was left penniless and alone. He finally returned home, ashamed. His father, who loved him unconditionally, welcomed him home and forgave him—just as our Father in heaven forgives and welcomes us.

Even our best friends will disappoint us from time to time because of misunderstandings, human folly, or circumstances beyond control. You can't depend too much on people because no other person can live up to your expectations at all times. But there is one friend who will never leave you, never let you down, and never quit loving you. His name is Jesus. It's important to keep that perspective because when tough times come—and they will come—you will need life's greatest companion to see you through.

8

Surrender in Daily Life

s you accept Jesus and receive forgiveness, your new life begins. Old things pass away. All things suddenly become new. Once you acknowledge that God is the captain of the ship, He sets a divine course to steer you through the troubled waters of daily life. You take on the role of first mate, following His direction and trusting in His wisdom. Imagine your Creator steering you each day in a direction that He purposed from the beginning of time. That is an awesome thought. All you have to do is surrender to His plan. But how do you surrender daily? It is an ongoing process that develops as you learn the best ways to talk to God, read His Word, and hear what He has to say.

The Little Things

For me, daily surrender involves waking up every day and, first thing, having a conversation with God. It doesn't have to be some kind of superspiritual conversation full of "thees" and "thous." Often, for me, it begins with something as simple as: "Good morning, Lord, and what are we doing today?" I find that in the morning my mind is clear and, so many times, I can hear His voice more distinctly.

These conversations often help me focus on tasks I need to do each day. God may bring a particular person to mind to remind me to make contact with someone. Sometimes my daily conversation with the Lord helps me find the wisdom to deal with situations that have otherwise perplexed me. Often I emerge from those conversations in a more reflective and optimistic mood. I always make sure to thank Him for all He has done and continues to do in my life.

If you can give the first ten or fifteen minutes of your morning to the Lord, either through prayer or reflection in God's Word, I promise you, your days will never be the same. Many say that they simply don't have the time for this brief conversation with the Lord, but you can always make time. When our children were younger, I often had my conversations with the Lord in the car after dropping the kids off at school. There are so many opportunities. I'll turn off the television at home or the radio in the car and just take a few minutes to spend time with the Lord.

It's not a difficult thing to surrender even the smallest things in daily life, not when you come to understand that God is concerned about everything that concerns us—even the mundane things that most people wouldn't even consider asking God about.

Years ago, when our kids were still little, I lost the car keys. I could not find those keys anywhere in the house. Finally, Rachel said, "Mom, let's pray. God knows where the keys are." I couldn't argue with that, so we prayed a simple prayer and reminded the Lord that we needed those keys. Moments later we found them hiding under a pillow in the den. Now that may not seem like a significant spiritual event, but God is concerned about the small things too. And even today, whenever we are looking for something lost or misplaced, my kids will ask the Lord to help us find it.

Psalm 34:19 says, "A righteous man may have many troubles, but the LORD delivers him from them all" (NIV). That verse tells me that every step in our lives has purpose. When you are living a life surrendered to the Lord, consciously aware of His presence and doing your best to live uprightly, He will involve Himself directly in ordering your steps.

The Ordinary Things

Surrendering to God is important for you to remain connected to God, but it also affects others. When you don't surrender, it impacts countless other people around you.

Billy Graham was saved in a small church one night, one of only a handful of people who answered an invitation to come to the altar. What if the minister had decided not to invite people to accept Christ that night? What if he had decided that most of the people in the church already had a relationship with the Lord and that it would have been a waste of time to give a salvation call? As a result of this man's obedience, not only was Billy Graham saved, but nations and kingdoms were shaken because this young man would eventually proclaim the good news to millions around the world.

Every day there are opportunities for ordinary people to be used by an extraordinary God. In the workplace, at the grocery store, and in your community, you can be used by God to encourage someone around you. If every believer would take the time to stop and listen to the Lord each and every day, the world we live in would be radically changed for the good.

The Big Things

Daily surrender can have a substantial impact even on something as secular and commercial as the fast-food industry. The family that created and runs the Chick-fil-A restaurant chain—one of the largest privately owned restaurant businesses in the country—follows a very successful business philosophy guided by Christian principles that put the Lord at the center of everything they do.

A devoted Christian since childhood, Truett Cathy grew up in a poor family during the Depression years and often helped out in the kitchen of his mother's boarding house in Atlanta. He later opened the Dwarf Grill, where he invented the boneless breast of chicken sandwich. The first Chick-fil-A opened in an Atlanta mall in 1967. Truett jokes that he went from being a man of paltry means to one of poultry means.

Truett Cathy says that his personal and business missions are both guided by his faith. The corporate mission is "To glorify God by being a faithful steward of all that is entrusted to us and to have a positive influence on all who come in contact with Chick-fil-A."

As part of that faith-based philosophy, Chick-fil-A, which now has more than 1,340 stores and annual sales of more than $2.2 billion, is the only national fast-food chain that does not open on Sundays. This day off gives its employees the opportunity to be in church and with their families and to simply take time to recharge themselves physically, mentally, and spiritually, says Dan. T. Cathy, Truett's son and current president and COO of Chick-fil-A. "We all need times of solitude and reflection and physical rest. I wish I could be wired 24/7, but God didn't wire our bodies to work that way," he says. "We need sleep and rest and worship. And we think our food tastes better on Monday because we are closed on Sunday."

Truett's devotion to Christian principles and being a "servant leader" led him to create foster homes for more than 150 children, a summer camp that has hosted more than 21,000 young people, and a college scholarship program that has benefited more than 17,000 students by giving out $1 million in scholarships each year. The company also sponsors marriage conferences for couples to help families stay strong. "The Bible teaches it's better to give than to receive," Truett says. "I find that to be very true. There's no way you can out-give God."

Truett and his family continue to live out their faith and model it every day. In 2002, Truett was asked to speak at a congressional hearing on "Oath Taking, Truth Telling and Remedies in the Business World." The hearing had been scheduled in the wake of the Enron scandal that raised concerns about the moral deterioration in corporate America.

At the hearing, Truett spoke as he always does, as a man of deep and abiding Christian faith. "I believe no amount of business school training or work experience can teach what is ultimately a matter of personal character," he said. "Businesses are not dishonest or selfish, people are. Thus, a business, successful or not, is merely a reflection of the character of its leadership. I'm deeply disturbed, as you are, by the lack of character I see in the marketplace. In order to satisfy the increased pressure for greater profits, some business leaders are making bad choices, which ultimately hurt thousands of employees, stockholders, and the economy."[1]

The Chick-fil-A founder believes that "there's really no difference between biblical principles and business principles. The Bible, which is a road map, tells a lot about how to operate a restaurant."

"We feel that by operating on biblical principles, we honor the Lord through our work," Dan explains. "We start with something good going on behind the counter and from there, brother, get out of the way! Something special's going to happen to customers when you've got people loving their work—it simply flows over the counter."

The Cathys say theirs is a "hospitality business" in which they treat people with care and compassion, according to their Christian beliefs. "Our external service quality is built on our internal service quality; we treat each other with respect and dignity, genuine love and concern."

The Foolish Things

As Truett Cathy built his fast-food business into one of the nation's most successful chains, he also served as a great role model for his children. "He taught us that you honor God by being excellent at the work He calls you to do," says Dan.

Today, Truett's son Dan runs the company under the same Christian philosophy, while Truett, now in his eighties, concentrates on philanthropic work and on his goal of living to be a hundred years old because "he heard that few people die after that age."

The Christian philosophy permeates all that the Cathy family does in their daily business and personal lives, which is one reason that their fast-food franchise is known for having some of the best benefits and most loyal employees and customers. Dan came on my show to talk about the role God plays in his daily life and how the strength of his relationship with the Lord helped him through an exceptional challenge a few years ago.

In the spring of 2001, Dan was taking a break from his corporate duties to burn some brush on his property. Having run out of diesel, his son had just poured gasoline on a pile when Dan lit a match to burn it. But as he struck the match, the gasoline fumes around him ignited. "I was about an arm's length from the pile. As I lit the match, the whole thing went 'wah-voom.' In a split second, I saw the flames erupt and felt this incredible wall of heat push me backward," he wrote with his wife, Rhonda, in *The Burning Brush Experience.*

It is one thing to surrender to God's will in your daily life when things are just humming along nicely. The real measure of our commitment comes when we stumble or hit a wall, or get handed a challenge that disrupts our lives and routines, and, in the worst-case scenario, threatens to alter or even end our lives completely. Dan T. Cathy had a life that was blessed in nearly every way, but one careless moment nearly ended it all. Yet he now says that being severely burned in that incident was truly "one of the highlights" of his life.

Dan says God used "the foolishness of men" to teach him some incredible things in that painful experience. "I learned to slow down, to look people in the eye, to enjoy their company, and to enjoy the moment more," he says. "I can identify with people who experience trauma in a much deeper and more meaningful way now than I could before."

Dan's face and hands were covered with second-degree burns, which meant that he did not have to receive skin grafts that would have been required for third-degree burns, but it was still an incredibly painful process because much of his skin had melted away. Yet he still kept his faith and his sense of humor. "I tell people that I got a $28,000 chemical peel, using five gallons of gas," he says.

He spent ten days in Grady Memorial Hospital's burn unit. Since he could not use his burned and bandaged hands, Dan spent much of the time listening to the gospels on compact disc. He said the stories of Jesus's teachings made him "painfully aware" that instead of studying and following the business philosophies of corporate executives, he would be better served to use Jesus as "an incredible leadership model for business."

Another lasting lesson Dan drew from his "burning brush experience" is that "God can enrich our lives even with the stupid stuff that happens to us. When you go through challenging experiences, I encourage you to catalogue and capture them because you can learn from them," Dan says. "I still have redness on the back of my hands, but it is just enough for me to see and say 'Thank you, Lord.' It has put my attitude and gratitude meter on steroids."

A big part of Dan Cathy's business is carry-out, so it is not a surprise that he feels he has benefited from several "takeaways" from the fires of his burning brush. "We talk about the prayer of Jabez, in which Jabez asks the Lord to expand or enlarge his territory. I now have a connection with people who have experienced burns and who have a more extended stay than just an overnight quick checkup at an emergency room," he notes.

One of his biggest takeaways is learning that "you don't have to go through an experience like this in a state of fear," he writes in his book. "I experienced comfort throughout the whole process. I had total peace, God's peace, even out in that field with the fire burning behind me. I knew even then that there's never a place I'm going to go that God is not already there."

The Broken Things

For some people there is no such thing as "normal" daily life. Yet those who accept the Lord as their Savior find that the power of surrender works for them on a daily basis. I have never met anyone quite like David Ring, but like everyone who has the good fortune to meet him, I feel blessed to have the experience. His life offers so many lessons for us all.

"I was born dead. For the first eighteen minutes, I lived without oxygen in my brain." It left him with cerebral palsy, a condition that affects his motor skills and speech but not his cognitive functions. "It is a miracle I'm here today. I'm supposed to be a vegetable," he told me. "But it's not over until God says it is over."

David has written of his life experiences and his daily surrender in *Just As I Am,* and he has told his story to Marcus and me and our viewers on *Celebration.* It is always fascinating to hear David tell his story because despite the challenges he has in speaking, there is just something mesmerizing about the experience.

He says that people throw away broken things, but God uses them. It took David awhile to learn that, but it has become the message that drives him to speak around the world. He tells people that when his brain was deprived of oxygen, he was afflicted with cerebral palsy.

"Strike one," he says.

Then when David was eleven years old, in 1964, his father died of liver cancer.

"Strike two."

A proud "mama's boy," David was only fourteen when his mother too died of cancer. He'd been heavily dependent on her as his "number-one cheerleader." She had encouraged and protected him from the emotional hurts inflicted on him because of his debilitating condition. "I felt she was the only one who loved me just the way I was. I got down on my knees and said, 'Please, God, don't take Mama,'" David remembers.

"That was strike three," he says. "I gave up. I wanted to die. I lost my mama and I had no one to go home to when somebody said I walked funny and talked funny. It was no fun to be made fun of. I laid in bed every night with tears rolling down my face, begging to die. I wondered why God didn't ease up on me and pick on somebody else.

I told my family members to give up on me. 'I'm a loser. I'm a triple loser.'"

David had taken on the victim's role, and most people couldn't blame him or console him. He was also angry at the Lord, but his sister begged and cajoled him to go to church. "I didn't want to go to church. I grew up in the church. My daddy was a preacher. I thought, if God loved me, why would He let such bad things happen to good people? If God loved me, why do I have cerebral palsy? If God loved me, why did my father have to die? Why did my mama have to die? Why? Why? Why?"

As David Ring often says, we all have our own stories of pain and grief. We have all been there. Each of us has questioned God's plan at some point. *Lord, if You love me, why? Why? Why? Why?* Even the Lord Jesus asked such questions as He hung on the cross. "My God, My God, why have You forsaken me?" (Mark 15:34).

With his father and mother gone and his body tormented by his condition, David felt lost and unloved. But then, kicking and screaming, he finally went to church.

"I went to church just to get my sister off my back. I sat down, and as the preacher got up to preach, I thought, *Man, I wish you would shut up.* But that night the preacher's words convinced me, for the first time, that God does love me and that He has a wonderful plan for me," David recalls. "For the first time in my life, I found out that I'm not okay, but that's okay because God loves me anyway. Nobody is okay, but that's okay, God loves them anyway."

That night David gave his life to the Lord Jesus and God changed his life. He took away David's old broken things and gave him new beautiful things. He became a new creature formed in God's likeness. "He took away my loneliness and gave me happiness," David said. "I didn't want to die anymore. I wanted to live. I still walked with a limp. I still talked funny, but, oh, the joy that floods my soul, it makes me whole."

The Lord works in unexpected and mysterious ways. For those who have heard David speak, God's plan for him is now clear and even seems obvious. But when David was still a teenager, lonely, in pain, and overwhelmed by his handicap, no mere mortal could have grasped the glory that awaited him once he surrendered his life to the Lord.

He notes that he was lying in bed, "minding my own business" in 1971 when God called him to preach. "I said, 'I can't preach. I talk funny. I walk with a limp. People can't understand me. I have cerebral palsy.'"

Of course, as David realizes today, it was not news to the Lord that he had cerebral palsy. But David was so surprised by this calling from the Lord that he seriously asked for confirmation. It came. David dragged himself out of bed, still in disbelief. He opened his Bible and found himself reading Philippians 4:13: "I can do everything through him who gives me strength" (NIV).

David would need all of the encouragement he could get from the Bible and other sources because as soon as he set out to follow God's plan for him, he ran into doubters and disbelievers, even among those who consider themselves believers. We say we believe and trust in the Lord, but often when His plan is beyond what we can envision, there are doubters even among the faithful.

Marcus and I experienced this same skepticism among our Christian peers when we tried to follow God's plan for us in Dallas. Some of the greatest Christian leaders in America said we would never make it. Some laughed at us and said we were crazy. The sentiment seemed to be that God's plan for us just didn't make sense. But the Lord doesn't always make sense. Sometimes He makes miracles.

Daystar became the second-largest Christian network in America because it was God's plan, not man's. The story of Daystar, like that of our friend David Ring, serves as a reminder that you should never let the Devil destroy your dreams when your dreams come from God. Whatever your dream from Him might be, follow His plan. Be obedient to it, and you will be as successful as anyone can be.

Marcus and I remember when David came to First Family Church and we broadcasted his sermon on Daystar. We said then that his ministry is so effective because he yields himself totally to the Lord and gives God the glory. It takes humility to accept that we are children in the eyes of God and that the Father's plans are often beyond our ability to understand.

David says: "You wouldn't believe the discouragement I got from the family of God. Many preachers told me I would never make it. They said, 'You will never get enough invitations to speak. Nobody will have you in their church.'"

The Lord always gets the last word in these cases. David has been spreading God's Word for more than thirty years now, speaking in more than six thousand churches, telling the good news that Jesus loves us. David is having the time of his life as an evangelist, which proves one of his favorite Bible verses, "But God hath chosen the foolish things of the world to confound the wise; and God hath chosen the weak things of the world to confound the things which are mighty" (1 Corinthians 1:27, KJV).

The list of things David Ring was never supposed to be able to do is quite long—and quite wrong. One of those things was that he would never be able to find a woman who would love him as a husband. His own family members told him, "David, don't even look for a wife. No woman will love you. You can't make a living for a wife."

"But in 1981, God found me a dynamo wife who loves me," he says with a grin.

Others said he would never be able to father children. David is now the father of four. "I can truly say they are my best friends. We are not only family, we are friends. Every time I look at them, all I can say is 'to God be the glory, with Him all things are possible.'"

In All Things

The challenges of daily life can be enormous. You will be frustrated. You will be discouraged. So stay on the daily Path of Surrender. Don't give up. Don't throw in the towel. Surrender to God's plan.

No one else can understand the depth of your pain, your frustration, your hurt, your anger. No one knows your story. No one has walked in your shoes. But know that we all have stories. You can't change what has happened to you, but you can choose how you respond. Seek to be a champion, not a victim. Surrender to God and stand back.

"If God can change my life, God can change your life," David Ring says. "If God can use me, God can use anybody. You don't have any excuse. Go and serve God with all your might. I am telling you, there is life on the other side."

Make surrendering daily a way of life. There are days that you will wake up and everything is right in the world: You feel good, things are going well on your job, with your family—and it's easy to surrender. It's easy to focus on God and the blessings of God in your life in those good times. But what about those days when you don't feel well and things are tough at work or at home? What do you do? You do just as you would do on the good days. You surrender those things to the Lord and trust Him to see you through. You may not have an immediate answer. You may feel all alone and as though your world is crashing in; but the truth is that you are not alone, and it's during these tough times that surrender is vital.

The Bible says to cast "*all* your care upon Him, for He cares for you" (1 Peter 5:7, author emphasis). I cannot imagine living in this world today and not having a relationship with God. You see, it's during the difficult times that He shows Himself strong. Just when you feel like giving up, He tells you, "I am with you always, even to the end of the age" (Matthew 28:20). Just when you feel like you don't have enough strength, He tells you, "My strength is made perfect in weakness" (2 Corinthians 12:9). And just when the stress is overwhelming you, He says, "Come to Me, all you who labor and are heavy laden, and I will give you rest" (Matthew 11:28).

You will make it through the difficult times, and when you do make it, you will look back and remember that had you not surrendered to God, you would not be standing where you are today.

9

Surrender in Loss

*A*s a little girl, I sang a Sunday school song that said, "Faith is just believing what God says He will do." Faith in God is the very bedrock and foundation that we live by. How do we surrender in faith when it seems our whole world is crumbling around us?

Years ago I did an interview with Pastors Steve and Becky Riggle from Houston. They had been on a mission trip to the Philippines, where they ministered in prisons with deplorable conditions. During one of their prison visits, a riot broke out. They were taken hostage. The prisoners who held them demanded a van from the guards so they could escape. They took Steve and Becky with them so they wouldn't be pursued.

The prison guards had no intention of allowing the prisoners to escape, of course. As the van was driving out of the prison, the guards riddled it with bullets. As gunfire poured into the van and the escaping prisoners died around him, Pastor Steve had this amazingly calm and positive thought: *The peace of God will see us through.*

He and his wife were both injured but, miraculously, they survived. Later, Pastor Steve told me he had always preached that God will give us peace even in the most difficult of life's circumstances. Still, he often had wondered just how that would actually play out if he ever came face to face with death. That day in the Philippine prison, God's protective love permeated the hearts of Steve and Becky. They later told me that they had no doubt that God was with them. In those terrifying moments, they were not afraid because His presence was so tangible to them.

The Loss of a Parent

Sometimes when I reflect on the success of Daystar, it strikes me that what makes it most remarkable is the collection of outstanding Christians with so many diverse talents who are part of our network. I think God truly is assembling some of His best and brightest under the Daystar umbrella. This really becomes apparent when they share their stories of surrender.

Joe Ninowski, our music director, who keeps harmony among twenty-four musicians and singers, was delivered to us as a gift from the Lord. When you hear his surrender story, you will discover that he feels the same way about us. Joe believes his arrival at Daystar is God's way of completing a dream that began with Joe's father.

Joe is a fantastically talented guy who leads our singers and the band. He writes many of our songs, plays the keyboard like no one else, and composes many of the scores for Daystar on-air promotions. Joe came to us after losing his father, an entrepreneur and Christian radio pioneer in Detroit, in a 1981 private-plane crash. Joe's father had just sold his Christian radio station and had plans to launch a Christian television network when the tragedy struck. Joe was afraid his father's dream had died with him, but the son's surrender to God's plan eventually led him to Daystar, where that dream was reborn.

Joe's parents are heroes to him. His mother, Linda, survived the horrendous displaced persons camps of World War II, which is where her family found themselves after miraculously escaping her native Ukraine following the Nazi invasion. With her own passion for music and singing, she watched over Joe's piano lessons faithfully.

Joe Sr., a blue-collar guy, furnished stability, levity, and financial provision. Joe Sr. knew the value of a strong work ethic. He had worked his way up from janitor to part owner of a tool-and-die company. He eventually created a business enterprise that included security equipment, oil, and broadcasting operations, all the while helping to grow a thriving church in the Detroit area.

"My parents are both true examples of surrender because of what they sacrificed and how they lived," Joe told me. "Both of them laid their lives down for their children. My mom had to overcome a lot of things culturally and emotionally after such a devastating childhood. My dad had served as a marine in World War II, and he also suffered a time of great disillusionment, but he went on to become a successful entrepreneur and devout Christian."

Joe's father, who never had a formal education, worked eighteen-hour days but always found time to read his Bible, even if it was on the streetcar going to class at the Henry Ford Trade School in Detroit. "He took the Bible for what it was," Joe said. "If it was in there, Dad believed it and lived it, period." That propelled him in his life and sustained him through World War II, when he saw many of his buddies die. After the war, Joe Sr. grew disheartened, especially after he lost just about everything in a failed business. He grew so despondent that he drove his car to the Ambassador

Bridge in Detroit and climbed on the ledge to take his life. But before he could throw himself off, he remembered his father telling him, 'Joe, man will always fail you, but God will never fail you.' "

Joe Sr. recommitted his life to God and began faithfully reading the Bible again, sometimes in lieu of sleep. While working long days, he was also active in the Full Gospel Business Men's Fellowship and a pillar of the Christian community in Detroit. His activism and faith led him to become a partner in the first twenty-four-hour Christian radio station in Detroit. The call letters were WBFG, "We Broadcast for God," and the name of the owner's company—this may surprise you—was the Trinity Broadcasting Corporation.

"Through the Full Gospel Fellowship, Dad became close friends with giants of the faith such as Demos Shakarian, Rex Humbard, and others like Pat Robertson and Kenneth Hagin Sr. The story goes that one day Paul Crouch called Joe Sr., saying that he was creating a Christian television network and that they wanted to call it Trinity Broadcasting Network," Joe says. "My dad had a great heart and so he told Paul, 'We are all on the same team,' and gave him permission to use the name."

Still, for years Joe's father had a dream of reaching millions of souls with his own Christian television network. He was working on that dream when he and his brother, Dan, and one of their executives, Dean Spencer, were killed after their private plane crashed in a heavy fog. Joe Jr. had just started his second semester at Oral Roberts University.

"My father always had an optimistic spirit. He'd wake us up many Saturday mornings with a home-cooked breakfast and John Philip Sousa marches on the stereo. He was a man of great integrity and love for God. I remember coming home from school and finding him on his knees crying, praying for the needs of people and nations. It would humble me that he had a heart like that," Joe Jr. says.

"Losing him was the hardest thing I'd ever encountered. He had been such a rock, and I never realized how much we leaned on his faith until he was gone. His death started me on my own journey of faith, and over the last twenty-six years, I have been learning the power of abandoning one's self to God," Joe says. "Until your faith is tested—as mine was when my father and uncle were killed—you never fully understand what is inside you or what it means to lay your life down."

Joe realized his father's life was one of continual submission as he tried to live by God's rules while working in a man's world. "He personified integrity and hard work, but it was how he completely gave himself over to God's character that has sustained me," Joe explains. "I saw my parents go through very difficult times and get back up and be stronger. They always taught us to treat people right. More is caught than taught, and nothing is more powerful than seeing the example lived right in front of you."

Joe Jr. had taken classical piano for ten years, which put music in his heart. He also has his father's pragmatic side, so he went on to obtain a marketing degree at Oral Roberts University. Both his music and faith drew him into the Christian music world and church leadership. Joe's work as a music-production contractor for Daystar impressed us so much that in 2003 we invited him to join us, even though we had no job description for him at the time. You might say that it was a match "made in heaven."

"As my wife, Sheila, and I sat with Marcus and Joni over lunch, and they invited me to join the Daystar team, I had an epiphany. I was overwhelmed, and tears began to flow as I realized that God was reconnecting me to my father's dream, which I felt had died with him all those years ago," Joe says. "Daystar is all about touching the world with good news, hope, and healing, and that was what my father's life was all about."

Joe Jr. was deeply saddened by his father's death, but eventually he came to surrender his grief and his father's dream to God's plan. At one point, he felt that dream was gone forever, but the Lord worked one of His long-term miracles to bring it back full circle, with Joe playing a critical role in its rebirth.

"My father's death became a spiritual seed. My learning to surrender gave that seed fertile ground, and God brought it to full bloom through Daystar," Joe realizes. "It took many years, some uprootings and replantings, but by committing myself to living for God, the dream lives on."

The Loss of a Spouse

We all face moments of crisis, though some are more fearful than others. The Word of God tells us that He knows our limits and will not allow us to bear more than we can stand. He won't allow anything to happen to us that's beyond our capacity to bear. The important part of the equation is to know how to surrender even when you don't understand what is going on around you or even when it makes no sense to you at all.

We are typically overwhelmed in crisis situations. Our brains cannot process what is happening to us. That's what makes it a crisis. So it is important to lock away in your mind now, before the crisis, that God will be there for you—if you surrender to His plan.

Bishop Joseph Warren Walker III, pastor of Mount Zion Baptist Church of Nashville, has a great way of reminding us that the Lord is always there for us, even in what seems like the worst possible times. "When you are down to nothing, God is up to something," he says. Bishop Walker speaks from experience. He went through one of the most tragic crises possible when he lost his wife, Dr. Diane Greer Walker, to cancer in 2005. "When other people can't pick your pain up on their radar, God knows exactly what you are going through. He can tell you the exact cause of each teardrop. He will send a divine prescription and speak a word, like medicine to your bones," Bishop Walker says.

During his wife's illness and after her passing, Bishop Walker hurt and grieved. "I would go home to my personal valley and minister to my wife and then preach hope to people while going through a personal hell. Even after she passed away, her spirit reminds me that I have to keep showing up."

Bishop Walker reminds us that Jesus was in pain on the cross, but He continued to follow His Father's will, and so must we all. God will turn it around, but He does it on His eternal timetable, not our earthly schedule.

"You may say you need a breakthrough by next Monday, but God says, 'Your emergency is not My emergency. I am not in your time; I am in eternity,'" Bishop Walker says.

In the tragedy of his wife's death, Bishop Walker certainly did not get the outcome that he prayed for. But he chose to learn from the experience and use his knowledge to serve the Lord.

"I'm much better now," he says. "I'm stronger. I'm wiser. Thank you for allowing me to go through this, God, for Your glory. I know pain and know what it is to be down to nothing. Everything we go through, every tear we cry—everything has purpose. You, too, will live on and declare the goodness of the works of the Lord."

I agree with Bishop Walker that another thing we need to keep in mind is that nothing in life just happens. Everything happens with purpose—on purpose—to bring forth the will of God in your life. "No matter what happens, you have to know that God is actively moving behind the scenes," he says. "God will be glorified, you will be edified, and Satan will be horrified. The Devil will never get the victory in what God has ordained for your life."

The Loss of Love

Bunny Wilson, founder and president of New Dawn Productions, wrote *Betrayal's Baby* to share with her readers what she learned about overcoming the bitterness of being betrayed by a trusted friend or family member.[1]

At a young age, Bunny, a small-town girl from the Midwest, fled an angry and bitter relationship with her mother. She moved to California and married a successful record producer and minister, Frank E. Wilson. They had six children and a good life, but Bunny discovered that she was still haunted by the lack of her mother's love. She found healing only through surrendering her shattered relationship to Jesus Christ. That surrender came after a spiritual breakthrough that finally allowed the healing process to take place. Bunny, who has been a guest on my show and is one of my mentors, warns that bitterness destroys while forgiveness heals and rebuilds.

We have all experienced betrayal of some kind. It is difficult to reach adulthood without knowing the sharp pain of a broken trust. Often, that experience becomes a touchstone of sorts. We engrave it into our psyches—remembering times, places, and the exact words that cut the bonds of friendship or family. We vow to never be so vulnerable again. But until we surrender to God the hurt and anger of a betrayal, we will never feel contented. That pain buries itself in our subconscious and impacts all future relationships unless we give it up to Him and commit to following the course set by the Lord.

Bunny reminds us that if we believe salvation is God's greatest gift, then submission to His will is the second greatest because it leads to salvation. Jesus did not want to die on the cross. He begged the Father, "Let this cup pass from Me" (Matthew 26:39). But He agreed that His Father's will should be done; and in submitting to God's will, Jesus bought salvation for our sins. We too must submit to God's will by surrendering our friendships to Him and then following the path that He sends us upon.

It is easy to write that and to say it, of course, but much harder to give up all the invested emotions and actually do it. Bunny acknowledges that her struggle went on for years and years. She and her mother were at odds early in Bunny's childhood and things only became more contentious as the years went on. "I adored my father, but he worked three or four jobs to provide for us. All I wanted was him," she said. For whatever reason, she and her mother never got along. She felt that her mother denied her affection and love. "She pushed me away, and I couldn't understand that," Bunny says. "I grew very bitter toward her. We were like fire and kerosene in the same house. When I was thirteen she slapped me, and I turned and slapped her back and said, 'I hate you and wish you were never my mother.'"

As soon as Bunny graduated from high school, she moved from the house and never returned. She was running from the anger and bitterness she felt for her mother—but she would never be able to get far enough away from home to leave the crippling hurt behind. It ate at her like an acid boiling within her mind, body, and spirit. Like many people, she carried the poison within herself and could not escape it until she surrendered to God's healing hand.

"I thought I could leave that behind, but I took it into relationship after relationship and it manifested itself in many ways," she says. "I found healing only in the Word of God. We say the Lord's Prayer: 'Forgive us our trespasses as we forgive those who trespass against us.' God forgives us as we forgive others. It seemed like I forgave my mother a thousand times, but every time I thought of her I got angry all over again."

Bunny realizes now that it isn't enough to say you forgive someone. You also must give up the right to judge that person. You have to surrender that to the Father too, just as Jesus did. The next step is reconciliation. You must go to the person, the friend, or family member who betrayed you, and attempt to bring peace. The idea is not to rehash or reopen old wounds, but to move the relationship to a new level by surrendering to God's will and letting Him lead you out of the bitterness and hurt. And you have to allow the Lord to work on His own schedule, in His own wisdom. Don't expect an instant miracle; wait for one that works over time.

Bunny remembers feeling a "cold sweat" on one of her early attempts at reconciliation with her mother. They hadn't seen each other for nine months. Bunny still burned from what she considered to be her mother's "ultimate betrayal." For a daughter to feel as if her mother doesn't love her, nor want her in her life, is debilitating at best. It's not natural for a mother to not love her daughter. She fought with the notion that she might be better off to simply shut her mother out of her life entirely and never look back. With that attitude, she met with her mother and told her that she wanted a better relationship. Bunny went through the motions of reconciling, but clearly wasn't ready to do what she requested from her mother.

Her mother wasn't ready either. "It set off all kinds of stuff inside her," Bunny recalls. "She talked to me for four hours, rehashing. I said to her, 'I came here to heal and learn how to love you. What do you want to do?' She looked at me with the eyes of a dead person and said: 'If I had to do it all over again, I never would have had you.'"

Bunny felt again like she'd been slapped. "I went to my car and cried out to God and said, 'How can she say that she wished she never had me—that she felt the world would have been better had I never existed?'" Feelings of rejection and betrayal again swept over her. She wept for the next three days.

Then she prayed for God's guidance. God commanded her to do exactly what Bunny did not want to do. "He said to call her and tell her you love her," she says, "and I obeyed. I called and said, 'I love you.' I had to. Jesus said, 'If you love Me, keep My commandments.'" Bunny did as He ordered, despite her reluctance and dread.

After saying what had to be said, Bunny put down the phone because she believed she should expect nothing in return. She released her mother of any expectations and surrendered their relationship to God. She acknowledged that her mother was not a villain and promised God that from that moment forward, she would love her unconditionally.

For the next year and a half, Bunny worked at loving her mother without expecting anything in return. It was definitely a character-building experience. I've heard it said that our mothers know how to push our buttons because they installed them. After that year and a half, her mother still had not responded to Bunny's efforts with either forgiveness or love. They were having one of their periodic conversations when her mother said something that in the past would have infuriated Bunny. But Bunny had been building strength in her commitment to God's plan for this relationship. She did not let her mother's words set her back. "People know how to get your goat, but they won't if you don't tell them where it's tied up."

Loving someone unconditionally breaks their hold on your hurt. You hurt because you love with expectation, but when you don't have expectations, you are free. "Just by doing what the Word of God told me, I was free," Bunny says. "I let God break the spirit of bitterness and anger in my life, and it flowed down and blessed me and my children, too."

That is an important point. Bunny's commitment to loving her mother unconditionally sowed seeds that flowered in her other relationships with her own children and friends. But it took a great deal of patience and commitment. Finally, though, Bunny came home one day and, to her joy, found an unexpected message from her mother on her telephone answering machine: "This is your mom. I want you to know I love you and I have always loved you—and you can believe that."

Bunny's gift of unconditional love allowed the Lord to work on her mother's heart. If you are hurting from the loss of love, you can make it through with God's help. There is hope when you surrender all to the Lord and wait for His guidance. Isaiah 41:10 says, "Fear not, for I am with you; be not dismayed, for I am your God. I will strengthen you, yes, I will help you, I will uphold you with My righteous right hand."

The Abundance of God

We are finite. We have limited knowledge and limited understanding. Yes, we have the Word of God. We have prayer. We have other believers to lean on and support us. But in the end, we are still limited, especially in comparison to God's infinite capacities. He knows all. He sees all. And He understands all.

My friend John Paul Jackson said recently that "God sees time past, time present, and time future all simultaneously." That is a profound thought, and it makes it all the more obvious that we need to surrender our faith in God even in times of loss.

I've heard many ministers criticize Job for his behavior as chronicled in the Bible. But Job is one of my all-time favorite heroes. Job endured the worst losses imaginable—losing his kids, his health, his wealth, and his self-worth. But even after all of that incredible misfortune, he boldly proclaims, "Blessed be the name of the LORD" (Job 1:21).

The story of Job is inspiring to me because we all have had so-called friends like his—the sort of false friends who condemn you in times of crisis and blame your misfortunes on a lack of faith. Sound familiar? Rest assured that Job's friends were wrong. Job had plenty of faith, and the test he would endure would bring a testimony for God's glory. That's not to say that God cannot use godly friends, because He will, and it is up to us to discern whether they are giving us godly wisdom versus carnal judgment. There are consequences to sin, but often trouble comes when we are most faithful too. No one has walked in your shoes, just as no one had walked in Job's shoes. God chastised Job's false friends. The Lord praised Job instead.

One of my favorite passages in this oldest book of the Bible finds Job questioning God about the bad things raining down upon him. Job has questions. He doesn't understand. He wants to know why all of this misfortune is happening to him. God answers Job—and what an answer He gives. I encourage you to read those passages (Job 38–42) in which God lays it out for Job, in effect saying: "Okay, Job, who are you to question Me?"

In those passages, Job begins to understand that the created does not question the Creator because we have limited understanding. God sees and knows things that we cannot fathom. God knew He would restore everything to Job and then double it. The Lord rewarded Job because he is a classic example of someone who never stopped loving and trusting God—even in the midst of the worst losses imaginable.

As Bishop Walker noted on our show, "The Devil launched a systematic attack" on Job, attacking him economically, sociologically, physiologically, and spiritually—in every possible way. "But God knew Job would make Him look good," Bishop Walker points out. Why will God trust you with trouble? Because He can see in you what you can't see in yourself.

In times of crisis, you should think of yourself as one of God's great oak trees. Lightning may have knocked you down above the ground, but below it your roots are just as deep in faith as that tree was tall. In Job 14:7 the Lord tells us, "For there is hope for a tree, if it is cut down, that it will sprout again, and that its tender shoots will not cease."

If God can see Job through and bless him in the end, I know that He can do the same for you.

10

Surrender in Failure

*W*e've looked at the incredible power of surrender in all sorts of life situations, yet I often hear from people who feel that somehow they have done things that are beyond God's power of forgiveness. Others have told me that not even the Lord could help them in their time of crisis. These are very dangerous lines of thinking. I want to help you understand that there is nothing God cannot fix, no addiction that He can't replace with love, no crisis that He cannot relieve. There is no sin that the Father will not forgive.

Dallas Plemmons

Few of us will ever face the inhumane torture and torment endured by evangelist Dallas Plemmons, founder of Dallas Plemmons Ministries, which has established churches, orphanages, schools, and support ministries in Haiti, Peru, India, and Ghana.

Dallas has brought me and my television audience to tears more than once with stories of the extreme crises that God allowed him to endure and overcome. His story is a tremendous example of the power of surrender in the most difficult and challenging situations. Dallas makes a strong case that God is willing to unleash miraculous forces when you give up your life to Him—even if you had been running from him before.

The story of his walk with the Lord begins with his childhood and the influence of his godly grandfather, who was a preacher. He rode a mule through rural areas of North Carolina and Tennessee so he could preach and minister to people there. But Dallas saw his grandfather mistreated for being a minister and as a result, Dallas ran from the Lord as a hot-tempered, hard-drinking young man. He released his anger as a professional fighter until he was forced to quit. He then enlisted in the U.S. Army and did tours in Japan first and later, in Korea.

Dallas found God in the most unlikely places and under the most difficult circumstances when he experienced things no human being should have to go through. Amidst unspeakable horrors many miracles occurred, according to Dallas, who wrote about them in his book *Hell in the Land of the Morning Calm.* If you ever feel you are in a situation so horrible and so intense that you can't hear God's voice and you feel abandoned, remember that Dallas was able to reach the Lord and He responded.

"I was running from the Lord. When you run from the Lord, it goes from bad to worse. I ended up an alcoholic, smoking three packs a day," Dallas recalls. At one point, he found himself drunk and sick in a foxhole after drinking "a big barbershop-sized bottle of Bay Rum After Shave Lotion because I couldn't find alcohol." There, he says, "I came to the end of myself. I couldn't stand it any longer. And I said, 'Lord, You have to do something for me.'"

Dallas said he had been running from God most of his life, but at that point he was running toward Him for the first time. The Lord responded by asking Dallas to preach. "I knew it was the will of God for me, but I didn't want to do it. But I said, 'Yes, Lord, I will do that if You will help me.'"

After telling the Lord that he would preach, Dallas remembers seeing a "big ball of fire swirling in the air" and hearing an explosion. It was at this point that Dallas had a "Damascus Road" experience like the apostle Paul in the Bible—Dallas encountered a living God and made the choice to surrender his life fully to God. "The next thing I knew a group of men was gathered around my foxhole. A couple had pinned my arms down because they thought I was hysterical. They were slapping me in the face. My company commander sent for the chaplain, who said I needed psychiatric treatment, so they shipped me off to Osaka General Hospital." They quickly discovered that Dallas wasn't hysterical or crazy. He'd been saved, and he was overwhelmed at the transformation.

In the weeks that followed, Dallas moved up in rank and became a platoon sergeant with the Army's 27th Infantry Division. He'd once been known for his foul temper, drinking, and fighting, but he won over his superior officers and his men with his total transformation into a Christian leader. His men tested him every possible way, but they knew that transformation was complete when one of his soldiers, a man named Marvin, spit in Dallas's face as he broke up a fight one day. Dallas says, "The Devil stood up on my shoulder and said: 'God doesn't expect you to take that.' I was getting ready to hit him, but a small voice said: 'You don't want to send it all down the drain for one punch do you?'" Dallas walked away instead of lashing out.

"The Lord may not come when you want Him, but He always comes on time," he says. That night Marvin came to Dallas's room. "I led him to Jesus and we became close friends. We traveled all over the islands together and worked with missionaries in our free time."

Miracle 1

Dallas experienced incredible hardships and tragedies during the Korean War, but he also seems to have been the beneficiary of several miracles. Early in the war he was at his Wolfhound Regiment's roadblock near a small town about thirty miles west of Pusan, when his vehicle came under fire from an enemy plane. A lieutenant was with him in the front seat, and eight other soldiers were in the back of the truck.

Their truck burst into flames after the first round of shots. It was rolling backward down a hill, so Dallas was preparing to leap out when he heard the lieutenant pleading for help. He couldn't move. His left arm was torn off and laying across Dallas's foot. His right leg was all but ripped off too. Dallas could see fist-sized bullet wounds in his back. Dallas jumped out of the truck as it rolled backward down the hill, still burning. He then ran around to the other side and tried to free the trapped lieutenant, but he couldn't get him out. The truck rolled into a rice paddy and stopped. All of the men in it were dead, including the lieutenant.

When Dallas told Marvin that he had been driving the truck as it came under fire from the airplane, his friend was mystified. "You couldn't have been driving the truck at that point," he said.

"Why not?" Dallas asked.

Marvin then took Dallas back to look at what remained of the truck. Three rows of bullet holes crossed the back of the driver's seat and two rows crossed its bottom.

Dallas wasn't even scratched.

Miracle 2

Dallas was leading a patrol in search of enemy soldiers in the mountains of North Korea when guerillas ambushed, firing at them as they went down a ravine. The Americans hit the dirt. Two soldiers were lying next to Dallas. One said they needed to get up and run or they would be killed. All three were preparing to do just that when the Lord spoke to Dallas and told him to remain where he was. "I told the soldier closest to me what the Lord had said, but he refused to listen. His response still rings in my ears, 'This is no time for that crazy religion! We've got one chance. And that's to get out of here right now.'"

Dallas stayed put, but the other two soldiers jumped to their feet and started running. The guerillas shot and killed them. Dallas didn't move—but only because he found that he was suddenly paralyzed. He could not even open his eyes. He thought he'd been shot in the spine, or that he was either dying or already dead. An enemy soldier walked up to him, kicked him, and rolled him over.

"Even though I had no bullet holes in me or blood on my body, the man thought I was dead," he says. "Another soldier came up and stood over me for what seemed like an eternity. But neither of them touched me. They just left and headed back up the mountain."

Dallas eventually made it back to the American camp. When he told his chaplain what had happened to him, the chaplain said he needed to see a psychiatrist. After several days of examinations, the psychiatrist gave him an envelope with his report and told him to take it to his battalion commander. He noted that he had not sealed the envelope, so if Dallas wanted to read it, he could.

Dallas read it. Much of it was medical terminology that he did not understand. But at the end of the report, the psychiatrist wrote: "I would like to suggest that somebody inform your battalion chaplain that there is a living God."

Miracle 3

Then in 1950, on the night before Thanksgiving, Dallas began his most harrowing trial. The North Korean army had been defeated by then, but unknown to his company, the Chinese had massed troops on the border. The surprise attackers descended upon his American soldiers. Dallas and his men were pinned down. He saw a night flare, felt a sting on the back of his head, and blacked out.

He awoke, freezing, in his foxhole the next morning. He heard yelling and screaming in Chinese. An enemy soldier appeared and motioned for him to get up. When Dallas rose to his feet, the soldier knocked him down with his rifle butt. He rose again only to be knocked down again. Finally Dallas got up and was ordered to join nearly eight hundred captured U.S. soldiers being herded down the road by the Chinese. All around them were the bodies of dead and mutilated Americans.

As the forced march moved north, the captured Americans came upon a truck loaded with wounded U.S. soldiers. "They were piled on top of each other like firewood," Dallas recalls. He and the other captured soldiers watched helpless and in horror as the enemy surrounded the truck, poured gasoline over the men in the back, and set them on fire. Dallas prayed for those soldiers in the truck, and he asked the Lord for strength to endure because he knew that the enemy was trying to break the spirits of him and his men. He vowed not to let that happen. And as they marched, he and his men became more determined to resist.

They were taken into China across the Yalu River separating Communist North Korea from Manchuria. They reached a Chinese military camp where Dallas and the other Americans were herded into a shed. They were packed together so tightly they had nowhere to lie down. Each morning the Chinese would come through and pull out the dead.

For some reason, the Chinese military leaders had mistaken Dallas for an intelligence officer. They claimed he had been captured with two others from that division, so they began torturing him, trying to get information even as they tried to get him to turn against his own country.

"They wanted me to make a radio broadcast accusing the U.S. of committing atrocities," he says. "I told them that they couldn't make me do that. I wasn't going to be a traitor."

The enemy tried to break him by strapping him to a chair and forcing him to look into bright, rotating lights while they played tapes of what they wanted him to "confess." He fought their efforts by filling his "mind and spirit with something stronger than anything they could do." Dallas began reciting every verse of Scripture he could call to mind. For three days, he was tied to the chair, deprived of everything but occasional sips of water. But Dallas used the Bible as his shield. Finally, they cut him loose.

"I could tell they were furious because it hadn't worked. They took me outside, spread-eagled me faceup on the ground, and tied my arms and legs to stakes," he remembers. "Then they drove a stake against the top of my head so I couldn't move and started water dripping from a tank onto my forehead. At first I thought it was nothing, but after five minutes those drops felt like stones hitting me in the head."

Once again Dallas countered their torture by calling upon the Lord. Every time a drop would hit him, he'd say the name of Jesus. As he did that, he says, "I was carried off into my own world where I wasn't even aware of the water anymore."

His resistance further angered his tormentors. They tied him facedown on the floor so that if he moved his hands or legs, he would strangle himself. In the process, they tore his shoulder out of its socket. He was in agony. Dallas begged God to let him die, but he refused to kill himself, even though his captors had made it easy for him to do. Finally he passed out. He awoke in a blackened cell, convinced that he was dying.

"I said, 'Lord, I'm coming home now' and He spoke to me clearly and said, 'No, not yet.'" Suddenly, his cell was flooded with the most beautiful light. "I could see the forms of angels, and then I passed out again. I was awakened again, but this time the enemy dragged me back to the American compound. I had survived."

Miracle 4

After several days the Communist Chinese led Dallas and the other prisoners out of the shed and began marching them in below-freezing temperatures through a narrow pass surrounded by steep, snow-covered mountains.

Dallas was walking with the other soldiers when the American in front of him fell to the ground. He'd been shot in the leg and went into shock. To keep him from being trampled and left behind, Dallas grabbed him and pulled him to his feet. The soldier took a few steps and fell. Again Dallas picked him up, but as he was helping him a guard swung his rifle barrel at the wounded man.

"I kicked the guard as hard as I could, then I ran and dove over the side of the mountain," Dallas says. "A large group of Americans followed me and ran and dove over the steep side of the mountain, tumbling down through the snow. The other American soldiers saw me and did the same. I rolled and tumbled head over heels into a narrow ravine where two mountains came together. When I hit the bottom, a body landed on top of me, then another and another until I was completely covered with bodies."

The Communist soldiers fired their rifles into the Americans. Dallas told the men to be still so that the enemy would think they were all dead. Finally, they stopped shooting, but to his horror Dallas realized that blood was oozing all over him. He could hear his fellow soldiers moaning and gasping. Afraid to move, he stayed where he was. And then there was nothing but silence.

When he finally crawled out from under the other men, he realized that he was the only survivor. He was freezing cold, covered with cuts and soaked in blood, but he was alive.

Miracle 5

"I fell on my knees and prayed. The Lord reassured me that He would not leave me," Dallas told me. "I knew that to survive I had to generate body heat, so I started climbing back up the mountain. I headed back up the road toward the Yalu River."

He surrendered not to the enemy, but to God. He walked and walked, letting the stars and the Lord guide him. For weeks and weeks he slept during the day, hiding wherever he could, living on raw rice and cabbage stalks, and then walking on in the freezing night.

"The Chinese had given me one of their quilted uniforms, which turned out to be warmer than anything our own troops were issued. When I stopped to sleep, I'd try to get enough leaves or soil or whatever I could find between me and the snow to keep my body heat from reaching the snow," he said. "We had been taught some survival techniques. I knew to eat the inside bark off certain trees. I'd eat that and every now and then I'd find a Chinese cabbage patch where I could dig the roots out and eat those. I found a flintlike stone and used that to skin the rabbits I could catch in the deep snow. I would skin and eat them raw, chewing the meat and spitting it out just to get the nourishment."

Dallas came upon a good Samaritan while trying to find his way out of enemy territory. The North Korean happened to be a Presbyterian Christian. He took Dallas into his home and, for the first time in many months, provided him with a hot meal and a warm bed. "But I left before the sun came up because I knew his family would be killed if anyone saw me," Dallas said. "I didn't want to endanger them."

The Lord guided him as he moved at night, until he finally came to the Yalu River. He could not cross on a bridge because the enemy would have seen him. Dallas remembers staring at the river and the mountain range behind it, wondering how he would cross the river and the range and get to the Americans on the other side.

"I said aloud, 'Lord, how am I going to get across the river and the mountains?'" His mind went blank, and suddenly he was aware that he was standing in another place, far beyond the river and the mountain.

Miracle 6

"I don't know how far south I landed, but I came to somewhere near the American position because I heard our artillery firing. It was daytime but I kept walking. I was wearing the Chinese quilted uniform by then, so I feared I'd be mistaken for the enemy and shot," he remembers. "Sure enough, as I approached the American compound, a soldier spotted me and shot at me. For the first time in my life, I was glad that one of our men was a lousy shot—either that or he was a very good one. He took out a piece of my ankle and brought me down, but as the soldiers approached, my South Carolina accent managed to convince them that I was one of the good guys."

Dallas recovered from his wounds and injuries and returned to the United States where he prepared for a life as a global missionary with his wife, Zoni.

You might think that this modern-day Job had endured enough trials, but Dallas would face more challenges. In 1966 he was praying at an altar on Lookout Mountain when the Lord told him that his missionary work was needed in Korea, the land of the morning calm.

Dallas followed God's guidance. Several months later he made it to Korea. He preached three times a day with the Prayer Mountain Conference of the Korean Presbyterian Church. His efforts were recognized by the chief of chaplains of the South Korean army, who invited him to speak to the men. Dallas had planned to spend a week preaching the gospel to the Korean troops, but during his visit with them, he was stabbed with a poison dagger by a Communist agent. Once again Dallas survived, returned to his pulpit—and by the end of the week, seventeen thousand South Korean soldiers had accepted the Lord.

If the stories of Dallas Plemmons don't convince you that God accepts you when you surrender to him no matter what you've done in the past, I don't know what will.

Dallas, who has been ministering for more than fifty years, says that no matter what happens to you, there is always "hope in Him." He continues, "There is no situation you can get into that He can't reach you if you will call on Him. Believe it, and receive it, and it will be yours."

Pat Summerall

The trials faced by Dallas Plemmons during the war years and after were not of his doing. They were crises that evolved from the torments of events much greater than any single man. But it is also true that the crises many people face are often created by their own bad judgment, poor decisions, and lack of faith. Amazingly, even when we bring the world down upon ourselves, God always stands willing to come to the rescue if we are willing to surrender ourselves to His will.

One of the most stirring examples of that is provided by a man who came to Jesus very late in life, almost too late. His story is fascinating because he was such a well-known public figure and celebrity, a "man's man," who, in reality, was living the reckless life of a man-child who refused to grow up.

Today, with his life surrendered to the Lord, Pat Summerall would be the first to tell you that he is an example of God's incredible capacity to forgive and to love. This renowned broadcaster and former athlete certainly also will admit that he hurt many people, including his first wife and children, while nearly destroying himself in the process.

For decades Pat was the signature voice for professional football. One of the world's most recognized sportscasters and pitchmen, he rose from poverty and a crippling deformity as an infant to become a multimillionaire and member of the American Sportscasters Association's Hall of Fame. His biography reveals his struggle with alcoholism and his self-indulgent lifestyle throughout his illustrious career. His is a story with lessons for all of us—because despite his hedonistic, ungrateful, and self-destructive lifestyle, Pat finally came home to the Lord.[1]

The Golden Boy

It is interesting that this man who became a "golden boy" first as an athlete and then as a sports broadcaster, was born with a deformity that very easily could have tormented him all of his life.

"I was born on May 10, 1930, with a bum leg, into a family broken and beyond repair," he notes in the first chapter of his autobiography. Initially, doctors felt he would never be able to walk normally since his leg was twisted backward. But a daring local physician tried breaking and turning the leg—an experimental procedure at the time. It worked so well that Pat was able to not only walk but also to become a superior athlete, excelling in football, basketball, golf, and tennis.

Pat's father and mother had separated before he was born, and neither his father nor his mother were there for him as a loving parent day in and day out. However, a loving grandmother, aunts and uncles, and other caring adults gave Pat the guidance and love that his parents failed to provide, so he grew into a good, hardworking student as well as an outstanding athlete in Lake City, a small, north Florida town.

The one thing Pat did lack was a strong religious upbringing, and that would contribute to his lack of a moral compass as an adult whose life seemed to be blessed in nearly every other way. After flourishing as an athlete in high school and college, where he played both football and basketball, Pat became a professional football player. He eventually landed on the New York Giants football team, where he became a star kicker. Just as his playing days were coming to an end, he lucked into a chance audition and won a broadcasting job with CBS Radio. The "golden boy" athlete moved rapidly up the ladder and the pay scale to become a pioneering television sportscaster and a wealthy man.

Along the way he'd married a Lake City girl and started a family—but Pat was anything but a family man. In fact, he took his family and his many blessings for granted. "Good things happened to me so fast that I didn't realize who was responsible," he says. "I thought it was all my doing. I was very self-centered and selfish. I took it for granted that I was always in the right place at the right time."

The good times rolled easily for Pat Summerall, and he rolled with them, neglecting his wife and children, womanizing and drinking and partying at every opportunity. As a celebrity, Pat was feted by men and pursued by women. His work required constant travel and entertaining. The party life replaced family life. Pat still had the competitive instincts of a professional athlete, and he fell into a pattern in which he and his drinking buddies—many of them also former athletes—would try to outlast each other at the bar. Their "last man standing" drinking binges dragged several of them deeper and deeper into alcoholism. Social drinking after work gave way to drinking in the afternoons and then the mornings too. Pat was a healthy, strong man who got away with abusing his body for many years.

But his body couldn't handle this lifestyle forever.

"My moral standards deteriorated and my work ethic was less intense. There were times people told me to slow down and take it easy, but I didn't think it affected my work ethic—though now I'm sure it did. That is one of the first evils that happens to you," he told me. "People did warn that I was losing control, but I didn't think they knew what they were talking about. I'd get mad at them."

Millions of viewers welcomed Pat into their homes as the voice of NFL football. His popularity brought lucrative endorsement deals and television commercials along with other opportunities for financial gain. Yet Pat tended to think these blessings were simply his due.

"I was so busy advancing up the corporate ladder and being part of television's number one sports broadcast team that I neglected my responsibilities as a father," he said. "Later I realized that one of the most important things any parent has to give is time, and I gave them no time. But I didn't realize that until I had overcome my addiction to alcohol."

The Intervention

Eventually, his self-indulgent lifestyle caught up with him. His drinking got so out of control that Pat found himself coughing up blood. Though he denied it, his ability to do his job had also declined. On the day after the 2002 Master's Tournament—one of Pat's signature broadcasting assignments and his most beloved venue—his former broadcast partner, Tom Brookshier, called with an unusual request.

"Brookie" asked Pat to meet him in a New Jersey motel to help him win over a client for his sports-marketing business. Sick and weary, Pat tried to beg off, but Brookshier would not have it. It all seemed a little suspicious to Summerall, in part because this hotel was not exactly the sort of luxurious place that Brookie would normally entertain a client.

When Pat entered the conference room for the meeting, he realized his suspicions were correct. Fourteen people were waiting for him, nearly all of them important figures in his life. Among those present were CBS president Peter Lund; PGA tour commissioner Deane Beman; Tampa Bay Buccaneers president Hugh Culverhouse; Pat's wife, Kathy, and several good friends; as well as his golf-broadcasting boss, Frank Chirkinian.

The person Pat did not recognize introduced himself as a representative of the Betty Ford Center. Pat suddenly realized this was an intervention. His concerned friends, co-workers, and family members had decided that Pat needed to enter the clinic's alcohol-abuse program, whether he wanted to or not.

It was a turning point in Pat's life, but at first he fought it intensely. "I was very angry. Most interventions are like that. I felt that other people had more problems than I did," Pat told me. "But then they read a letter from my daughter, my oldest child, in which she said she was ashamed that we had the same last name."

His daughter's words burned through Pat's resentment at that meeting. He agreed to board the plane they had waiting to take him to the Betty Ford Center. "I thought, if all these people think I have a problem maybe I do have a problem. I began to listen—and thank goodness I did," he says.

The normal length of the alcohol-abuse program at the Betty Ford Center is twenty-eight days, but Pat had to stay for thirty-three because he spent the first few days working off his anger and denial. The message had to sink in. Pat's athletic and broadcasting careers had him on the fast track for so long that he'd rarely taken any time to reflect. Now, he did, and what he saw was deeply troubling.

The Lord's Word

The Betty Ford Center allows only two books in the rooms of its residents. One is an Alcoholics Anonymous manual. The other is the Bible. Once he calmed down and accepted that he had a problem, Pat began looking for answers in the Bible. It was the first time he really studied God's Word, and it was a revelation for him.

"I had so many questions about life and conscience. Who was responsible for me making the right decisions? So many questions were answered in the Bible," he says. "I realized that there was a higher power who could help me with this addiction. I saw that there was a right way."

In the Bible, Pat found the meaning, direction, and spiritual and moral guideposts that his life had so sorely lacked. As he read the Lord's words, he found that his desire for alcohol faded and then disappeared. "When I returned home, I realized that I had overcome the desire for alcohol."

Two weeks later Pat asked Dallas area minister Claude Thomas to baptize him. "I don't know exactly when Jesus took up residence in my heart, but I know it happened," he says. "I do know that when I got out of the water at my baptism, I had a totally different feeling. I felt lighter and happier. I knew what they were talking about when they said 'reborn' or 'born again.' I realized what it was all about."

Pat was reborn as a new creature in Christ Jesus. His life had been decadent and out of control, but there is nothing God cannot fix. He replaced Pat's addiction to alcohol—one of the worst possible forms of addiction—and the hedonistic lifestyle with His love. God took control of Pat's life and guided him on a new course.

But Pat had yet another crisis to face. "Soon after I got out of the Betty Ford Center, our family doctor told me that my liver was severely damaged. I didn't realize how serious it was. But after a couple years, I started to lose stamina and gain weight. I realized I was going down hill pretty fast and something had to be done about a new liver," he recalls.

Pat quickly became very sick, which qualified him for the liver donor program at the Mayo Clinic in Jacksonville, Florida. His health deteriorated so rapidly that he nearly died before a replacement liver could be found. "I'd almost given up hope, but I always had faith," Pat says.

God sees past, present, and future simultaneously. The Lord looked at Pat and saw that he would be faithful in his later life, so he was given the opportunity to use his celebrity for a higher purpose, to share with others the power of the Lord Jesus.

"I was lying in bed at the Mayo Clinic waiting for the liver transplant and having a tough time thinking about the fact that someone had to die for me to get a donor liver. I kept wondering why I should get another chance after what I'd done with my life. John Weber, the chaplain of the Dallas Cowboys, came to visit me along with minister Claude Thomas. I asked them why they thought I should get a second chance and, as if they had rehearsed it, they answered together: 'God is not through with you yet.' "

John Weber then added another compelling thought that Pat Summerall has never forgotten. "He said that now two people had died for me to live—the young man whose liver I received, and, of course, Jesus Christ."

Pat was humbled by those thoughts, and as he went into the operating room, he surrendered his life and his future to whatever God had in mind for him. He had no idea what that might be, but he vowed to do whatever he could to serve the Lord. His surgery and recovery went so well that his doctors would later describe him as "the perfect transplant."

I think God would describe Pat as a perfect example of the power of surrender and of showing the Lord's unlimited capacity for forgiveness. If you surrender your life to the Lord, He will find a purpose for you. Pat Summerall is in a unique position to reach other men and women who have lost their way to alcoholism or hedonistic lives. He has become a soldier of Christ.

As Pat Summerall and Dallas Plemmons discovered, the journey of faith and surrender is not an easy one. You may feel at times that you are dying a little each day. But you can hold on to the knowledge that Christ lives within you and, if you surrender, He will guide you so you are doing exactly what you were created to do. Surrender brings satisfaction beyond comprehension. In the state of surrender comes the realization that this earthly life is just a dress rehearsal for the everlasting life to come. Everything that happens here prepares you for eternity. Best of all, it's not too late to get right with God.

11

Surrender That Saved the World

I could not write about the power of surrender and its influence over my life without drawing lessons from the ultimate surrender. If it had not taken place a little more than two thousand years ago, we would have no promise of eternal life. Your life on earth is important, and surrendering this life to God will bring you fulfillment and joy beyond comprehension—but it is vital for you to understand that this life is just a prelude to the everlasting life to come.

The Word of God opens with these words: "In the beginning God created the heavens and the earth" (Genesis 1:1). There, our story begins. God delighted in His creation of Adam and Eve. He longed for fellowship with those cast in His image, which meant He could not force them into a relationship with Him. He had to give them the freedom to choose His love.

To make a very complicated story simple, Adam and Eve sinned—and with their fateful choice, eternal life for all mankind was lost.

In His great love, God devised a plan for our redemption. The first prophecy of man's redemption would be directed at Lucifer, who had tempted Adam and Eve to sin in the Garden of Eden. "And I will put enmity between you and the woman, and between your seed and her Seed; He shall bruise your head, and you shall bruise His heel" (Genesis 3:15).

This is the first promise we have from God that the serpent's head will be crushed and that the woman would play a role in this. As a result, mankind would have the opportunity for redemption and eternal life. All Christians know well the story of Jesus's miraculous birth. We also are familiar with the Old Testament prophecies written hundreds of years previously that foretold where He would be born, the purpose of His birth, and how He would die. These stories with so many intricate details leave no doubt that Jesus is the promised Messiah and Savior of the world. With that historical knowledge, we understand why Jesus, being fully God and fully man, would have to surrender His life for ours.

Jesus's surrender of surrenders occurred in the Garden of Gethsemane, which is a holy and inspiring place. My recent visit to Israel with members of my family and the Daystar team was a profound experience for me. We toured many historic biblical sites in the Holy Land, but the place that had the biggest impact on me was this place where Jesus might have prayed His final prayer of surrender.

When you think about the suffering Jesus endured on the cross of Calvary, you must never forget that, as Isaiah tell us, "He was wounded for our transgressions, He was bruised for our iniquities; the chastisement of our peace was upon Him, and by His stripes we are healed" (Isaiah 53:5). The physical pain that Jesus endured on the cross was tremendous, but I believe the mental anguish He experienced in the Garden of Gethsemane was maybe greater than the physical pain He knew was coming in His final hours.

I learned on our trip to the Holy Land that *Gethsemane* means "oil press." I saw the garden, and that translation makes sense to me, for the garden is surrounded with majestic olive trees that date back over two thousand years.

In Luke 22 we are told that Jesus went to the Mount of Olives to pray, as was His custom. His disciples followed Him there and He told them: "Pray that you may not enter into temptation." Jesus went to be alone. He knelt and prayed, saying: "Father, if it is Your will, take this cup away from Me; nevertheless not My will, but Yours, be done." Then an angel appeared, giving Him strength. "And being in agony, He prayed more earnestly. Then His sweat became like great drops of blood falling down to the ground" (verses 39–44).

As I stood in the garden, I considered that powerful image. It struck me what a powerful and important moment this was. I could not imagine what was happening physically to Jesus as His sweat became drops of blood. I believe that Jesus died in the Garden of Gethsemane—not a physical death, because that would come hours later. I believe He died emotionally in the garden due to a broken heart. In those terrifying moments, Jesus had the weight of mankind upon His shoulders.

Human Suffering

The Garden of Gethsemane seemed to cause many of us on that trip to reflect on our own humble sufferings and subsequent surrenders to the Father. All of us could sense the despair and pain Jesus must have felt. We were all grateful, knowing that because He had surrendered in the very garden where we stood, we had the hope of eternal life. As my traveling companions and I stood there in the garden, we talked about the anguish Jesus must have felt over two thousand years ago as He knelt in the same spot. It was a very emotional experience for that reason, particularly for a few of our people whose life journeys have been long and arduous.

Samantha McNeal, who has been my executive assistant for ten years, was one of those deeply touched by our visit to the garden. She told me that our visit to Gethsemane was a healing experience for her. Sam, as I call her, experienced extreme levels of mental anguish during a nightmarish childhood, though to know her today you would never believe what she has been through.

I tell my children that you never know what trials and difficulties those around you have faced. I think of that whenever I'm tempted to have a pity party because something hasn't gone right. If we were to stop and listen to the stories of those around us, we would come back with a thankful heart. There's always someone who has been in a worse predicament than we have, and as we get the focus off "self" and live our lives to honor God, all of a sudden, our problems aren't so bad after all.

I have been close to Sam for many years. It is amazing to me that she survived her horrific childhood, and even more striking that she functions at a high level, handling her work responsibilities along with being a wife, mother, and grandmother. Her life reminds me that sometimes we have to look for miracles no further than the person standing next to us. Sam is a miracle, and the miracle she experienced is attached to her Savior—but none of it would have happened if Sam had not been willing to surrender everything.

Ill-Fated Life

Sam grew up with two brothers in a surreal, but outwardly normal, environment that seems drawn from a horror novel. Her handsome father was a laborer with a major tire company. Her mother was a beautiful and glamorous woman. They lived in Akron, Ohio. Their family probably appeared to be the middle-American ideal. Yet, behind the facade, their household was a battleground. Her alcoholic father, who kept loaded rifles and pistols all over the house, physically abused his wife and tormented the children with the constant threat of violence.

"He would wrap coat hangers around my mother's neck and try to choke her," Sam told me. "My mother once looked at a self-portrait of my father that he'd hung over their bed and told me: 'If Satan has ever roamed this earth, he did it in the form of your father.'"

I can't imagine being a child burdened with that image of a father or growing up with a mother who was terrorized day in and day out by him. Sam's father rarely turned his rage upon his children, but when he did, the violence was staggering. "My brother Larry was going into his senior year when my father beat him up so badly my mother was afraid he would beat him to death," Sam recalls.

Her mother sent Larry to live with his grandmother in Alabama after that, but Sam and her brother Terry were still vulnerable. Her father's drinking continued. Often he would come home drunk and threaten to shoot them all. "One time Terry and I were trying to wrestle a rifle away from him because he said he was going to shoot our mother. We were struggling with him in front of a picture window, and we just looked at each other as we had the same thought. Without a word, we pushed him through the window and grabbed the gun," she says.

In another incident a few years later, her father came home drunk and began waving a pistol around, threatening to kill Sam's mother. "It was a German Lugar," she recalls. "He put a clip in it and I heard it click. Terry and I told my mother to leave and she ran out the front door. Terry told Dad that he didn't want to hit him but he would if he tried to go after my mother. My father started to go after her, and Terry knocked him out."

Sam's father was a womanizer who was very jealous of his beautiful wife. He tapped her phone and refused to let her drive a car. He put candle wax on the bottom of her high heels so he could tell if she went out when he was away. He tried to control her through fear. "I came home from school one day, and my mother was standing at the top of the stairs. She was soaking wet, fully clothed. She told me my father had tried to drown her in the bathtub. He'd held her down in the water until she nearly passed out, and then let her up and laughed," Sam remembers, shuddering. "There were times in the past he had broken her nose and cut her with a knife. He was a very evil man."

There was other evil around. Sam was molested by a male trusted by the family when she was five years old, adding that torment to a young life spent in a house of horrors.

Her mother tried to protect Sam and her brothers. She had read the Bible through several times, watched Billy Graham crusades on television, and sent them to a small Baptist church down the street. But Sam's mother could not understand how to surrender her life to God. Instead, she gave up.

Sam was fifteen years old when she awoke on a Sunday morning to the screams of her brother Terry. "I was in a real deep sleep. I heard Terry scream and the sound of breaking glass. I ran into the bedroom next to mine and there was my mother. She was laid out in a housecoat, and my brother was crying and screaming. He had found her emptied glass bottle of pills and thrown it against the wall, shattering it. My mother's face had turned blue, and at first I thought my father had beaten her to death and I wanted to kill him," she confesses. "I went running through the house looking for him, but we found out later he was out drunk, with another woman."

In her desperation, Sam went back and tried to revive her mother. "I straddled her body and tried to revive her. I blew into her mouth without holding her nose closed at first, and I'll never forget the coldness of the air that came through her nose onto my right cheek," she says. "I kept it up for a few minutes, but I knew in my heart that it wasn't working. My brother had called the paramedics who came and took us out of the room."

Sam's mother left two suicide letters. One was to Sam. It said that she should go live with her mother's sister in Alabama, away from her father. In the other letter to Sam's older brothers, her mother explained that she could no longer take the emotional and physical abuse from her husband.

Sam did not go to live with her aunt in Alabama. She wanted to finish high school with her friends, so she stayed with her father, whom she hated as much as she feared. "I developed a burning hatred for him that really consumed my mind for years and years," she admits.

Her father continued drinking and womanizing, often staying away from home for days. Sometimes he'd bring home women who were only a few years older than his daughter. He was not violent toward Sam, but he was emotionally abusive. "He didn't chase me with the guns anymore. But he would chase me around the dining room table with a broom, calling me Judas," she remembers. "Apparently he felt I had betrayed him to my mother in some way. He also would come home drunk and wake me in the middle of the night and badger me. He would say that I knew things about my mother that I wasn't telling him."

Not surprisingly, Sam rebelled. When her father would not give her money for clothes, she asked her friends to rob him. "If he struggles, hit him in the head with a baseball bat," she told the friends. "I want him dead anyway." Fortunately, they ignored her.

At the age of sixteen, Sam began thinking of committing suicide. One night while drunk, she put a pistol to her head, but a friend snatched it away. She fought similar impulses for many years after that. Sam was eventually diagnosed with bipolar disorder, also referred to as manic-depressive illness. She was in and out of mental hospitals throughout her late teens and early twenties. She spent those years in bad relationships, abusing drugs and alcohol. She married, got pregnant, and divorced.

Blessed Redemption

Sam was a single mother, raising a two-year-old daughter, when her brothers convinced her that she needed to start taking her child to church. "I took her to this little Nazarene church in Kenmore, Ohio, with the intention of just giving my daughter a religious foundation," she told me. "But then the pastor gave an altar call and I felt compelled to go up. I gave my heart to the Lord that day."

Sam began to emerge from the darkness after first surrendering her life to God in 1974 at the age of twenty-six. A dramatic and inspiring transformation was underway. In 1979 Sam married Steve, who is still her husband. With the Lord guiding them, Steve, who worked for James Robison's ministry, walked Sam out of her pain and misery toward a new freedom in Jesus Christ.

While traveling with Steve in Florida, Sam went to an evening church service and surrendered again during an altar call that forever changed her life. "I was skeptical but I heard the voice of the Holy Spirit saying that I had to have childlike faith. He said, 'Do not be afraid. I will in no way cast you aside. Ask what you would of Me now and I will do it. I bid you come now.'"

Sam had never experienced that sort of church service. She felt the power of God. Raising her arms, she asked God: "Deliver me from this spirit of suicide and severe depression, and I beg you to deliver me from manic depression."

She felt a real hand come up from her brain. Next she had a sensation of warm oil pouring over her. "I could feel a hand that passed through my mind and cleared out all the confusion," she explains. "And when I got up, it was the first time in twenty years that I could think clearly. The garbage and mental torment of severe depression were gone. After that I never had another mood swing or any of the problems associated with bipolar disorder or manic depression. It has now been eighteen years, and I no longer take any medication. This truly is a miracle that only God could perform."

Sam, who became an ordained minister in the Assemblies of God International in 1990, was well into her thirties before she could find the strength to do something that she never thought would be possible—forgive her father.

She had tried many times in the past, but the bitterness and anger and hurt always blocked the way. "Before, I would go to the Lord and pray and talk about forgiveness, but when I got to my dad, I had a difficult time. I would say, 'Forgive him,' then I would flash back to the abuse of my mother and my brothers and me, and so I would have to start the process all over again," she says.

"When I first became a Christian, I asked the Lord what I needed to do to forgive him once and for all," Sam recalls. "The Lord said 'Sam, you are forgiving with strings attached.' I asked what He meant, and I felt the Lord say, 'You are forgiving with the expectation that he is going to change and treat you differently. You have to forgive him with no expectation that he will change. Then let Me work with him.'"

Slowly, Sam came to understand that forgiveness is a process and that sometimes you have to forgive through gritted teeth. She took the Lord's words to heart, however, and slowly began processing them through her mind by reading the Bible. As she did that, it dawned on Sam that for Jesus to forgive her for all of the things she had done in her years of drinking and doing drugs and running around, she had to forgive others, including her father.

As she learned to surrender her anger and bitterness toward her father with no expectation that he would change, she found herself even closer to God. "I felt the Lord calling me to become an evangelist, and when I did that, my father would ask me if I'd been out preaching. He was in his eighties, and he had started watching Christian television."

It was around this time that I met Sam, and we became fast friends. She told me her incredible story of redemption and how she had worked to forgive her father for the terrible things he had done in his drinking days.

Then one day I had this vision of Sam and her father coming together in a moment washed with the light of total forgiveness. I saw her father accepting the Lord as his Savior if she gave him a simple plan for salvation, which was another of Sam's heartfelt dreams. I called her and told her about what I'd seen just as she was preparing to visit with him. Sam was thrilled by the encouragement my dream gave her.

She went to visit her father at his mobile home in Alabama and worked up the courage to ask him if he was ready to accept the Lord. "I told him that Jesus loves him and that He would forgive him and relieve him of all his guilt. 'We are all sinners,' I said. 'We just need to ask Jesus to forgive us and come into our hearts and wash us with His blood.' " Then she popped the question: "I said, 'Dad, would you like to accept Jesus Christ as your personal Savior?' and he said, 'Yes, honey, I would like to do that.' "

When Sam offers her testimony to others, she tells them that we have to look at the bigger picture instead of focusing on whatever pain we have experienced. She wants us to understand that sometimes we have to go through pain to get to God's glory.

Sam and her father went through the depths and the darkness before finding themselves in God's grace. She thinks of that sometimes when she reflects on all of the terrible things she went through. "The bigger picture for me is that if my friends had hit my dad with the baseball bat, I never would have had the opportunity to lead my father to Him. I know now that God had a plan for me."

During our visit to the Garden of Gethsemane, Sam and I talked about her journey from darkness and pain to the Lord's blessings. She reflected on the trauma and the emotional struggle that Jesus must have gone through to make the choice of giving over His will to that of His Father. We talked about the fact that He sweated drops of blood as He contemplated what His Father wanted Him to do.

Sam told me that she identified with what Jesus was going through emotionally and what His inner battle must have been like as He asked His Father to let this cup pass from Him. "Jesus didn't want to accept and go through with what was expected of Him," she reflects. "And for a long time, I did not want to forgive my father for what he had done to my family. But in the end, I accepted God's will and His wisdom. I forgave my father and I walked him to the Lord. I believe now that God can take the worst of life's situations and turn them to good."

Every day of our lives, we have to make decisions on whether to follow God's plan or our own, just as Sam had to decide whether to carry a grudge to her grave or to forgive someone who had tormented her family. In the end, she surrendered her right to hold onto that grudge. She chose God's will. She picked up the cross of Jesus and denied herself in order to follow Him.

"We tell people to have faith, but in highly emotional situations like that, it is not so easy," she says. "I think with forgiveness especially, the biggest struggle is surrendering to God's will. I wanted to hold on to anger because of the way I was treated by my father. Then, I thought of what went on in the mind of Jesus as He battled with His emotions in the Garden of Gethsemane. He finally realized it was more important to obey His Father and to follow His will than to give in to His own fears and sorrow."

Benita Arterberry Burns

Our music director at Daystar, Joe Ninowski, had worked with one of the most gifted singers I have ever met: Benita Arterberry Burns. Joe had worked with Benita on some mainstream commercials and jingles, and he suggested Benita for singing our opening of the *JONI* show introduction that we were producing for television. Benita and I instantly became friends and kindred spirits. We sometimes kid each other that although we may not have the same skin color, we must be from the same tribe because we feel such a connection.

It was not long after meeting her that Joe and I felt Benita was destined to be a part of the Daystar Singers, and she joined us with her melodic, perfect-pitch voice. When you listen to Daystar worship CDs, you can hear Benita's beautiful and anointed ad libs and vocals. Later in our private conversations, I learned some of her life story. I was amazed at God's grace in Benita's life. I could see the Lord's hand as she wanted more than anything else to surrender her gift to the Lord, offering every talent she possessed to be used for His glory.

Benita had also joined us on this trip to the Holy Land and the Garden of Gethsemane. It was her second time there with us, yet she was again moved by the experience. Benita shared with me in the garden that while on her knees praying with the rest of our group, she realized this was the first place that Jesus in His final days shed His blood. We were all emotional, thinking about His sacrifice, but once we were there, we were all overwhelmed. Benita mentioned to me that this was the site of our Lord's ultimate surrender and the greatest test of His will.

She said she was reminded in the garden of how our Lord must have suffered as He pondered what was about to take place. She marveled at how He had the courage to say to God, "Not as I will, but as you will" (Matthew 26:39). She was so thankful for God's love and forgiveness in her life as she recounted the struggles of having tried to commit suicide at age fifteen, marrying at an early age, becoming a teen mom, then a single parent, and being in and out of relationships, wondering what her purpose was in life.

How was it she would eventually be blessed with the singing ability that would win her Cleo and Emmy awards? she wondered. Or in becoming a finalist on *Star Search*? What a mystery that these were answers to her prayers, but also the very things that for a time she wanted more than the Lord. She felt like the prodigal daughter, but then she realized her childhood vision from God had kept her through it all and led her to this place in time. Humbled by the goodness and mercy of God, she offered a prayer of surrender to the Lord and asked God to let her sing for him for the rest of her life.

And God was faithful. He used Benita's gift for music and brought her into work where she could praise Him through the day. Benita joined us at Daystar, and now her voice is heard around the world as she sings a message of hope, love, and restoration. Benita will tell you: "Know that no matter where you are or what you have done and what has happened to you, this too shall pass. God will do things for you that you cannot even imagine. He knows you, He knows everything about you. Don't try and fool God. Don't play around with God. Surrender to Him and He will guide you to the peace that I have found."

God's Presence

As Benita shows us, surrendering to your Creator does not guarantee that your life will be a bowl of big juicy cherries. You will still face challenges. But surrendering to Jesus and the Father does come with this guarantee:

God will be with you even when life is the pits. And, for a true Christian, that is more reassuring than springtime.

Who would know better how to use us for this life than our Creator? He is the One who has uniquely gifted us. The One who sees the sparrow fall and knows every hair on our heads. Who better to decide what is best for us in this life?

Many people can't follow their God-given destinies because they don't give themselves up to His will. They know Him. They accept Him. But they don't yield to Him. The paralyzed motorcyclist who came to Betty Baxter is an example of this. He had given his heart to Jesus, and then got in line to be healed. But when it came to committing his life to Jesus through surrender to His will, he backed away. He wanted the Lord's blessings without fully committing.

The Bible tells us that Jonah did much the same thing. Jonah was one of the greatest preachers of his time. He must have been amazing, since he once preached to an entire city and all its people repented. But when God told Jonah to travel to the distant city of Nineveh and to warn the people there that God was angry with them, Jonah instead ran away in the opposite direction. He fled all the way to the coast of what is now Israel and the port city of Joppa, now called Jaffa. He boarded a boat and sailed out into the Mediterranean Sea.

Getting into a boat isn't the smartest move when you're on the run from God. God whipped up a big storm that rattled the small ship's crew so badly that they began throwing things overboard. Somehow Jonah slept through the first few minutes of the storm until the captain of the boat woke him up. He demanded that Jonah start praying for God to save them from the storm. Meanwhile, the sailors on the boat took a vote and decided Jonah was to blame for the storm. They began interrogating him, wanting to know what he had done to put God in such a stormy mood.

Jonah replied, "I am a Hebrew; and I fear the LORD" (Jonah 1:9). Knowing his own guilt, he told the men to throw him overboard to stop the storm. At first the sailors refused. They tried to keep rowing instead, but the storm only got worse. Finally, they asked God's forgiveness and threw Jonah overboard.

The storm stopped immediately—and we know what happened to Jonah. As the song says, "He made his home in that fish's abdomen." God sent a big fish that swallowed up Jonah. For three days and three nights he sat there undigested and in the dark. Finally, Jonah took the hint and prayed to God, asking forgiveness and promising to do whatever God told him to do.

God is forgiving. He sent the big fish to the shore where he spit out Jonah onto dry land. This time Jonah headed in the right direction, toward Nineveh.

If you run from God's will, you too will pay a price. God knows things we don't know. He sees across time, into the past and present and future. We may not always understand what is going on in the here and now, but we can trust that God has a plan for us. That is faith. Proverbs 3:5–6 says, "Trust in the LORD with all your heart, and lean not on your own understanding; in all your ways acknowledge Him, and He shall direct your paths."

We are finite and God is infinite. He is all-powerful, He is omniscient, and He is everywhere. How can we understand Him who is beyond us in every way? We can't. We have the Word of God, prayer, and the fellowship of others—and that is enough. In the life to come we will have a greater understanding than we have on this earth, but for now we have faith.

God's Plan for You

The message of surrender has become even more real and more powerful to me as I've taken you on this journey to share my personal stories and those of others I've worked with and interviewed over the years. It strikes me that there is a crimson thread of redemption woven through each story and each life. God creates a beautiful tapestry of purpose for all who make the decision to surrender.

After you've read the stories here and reflected on your own life, the questions surely arise: Have I truly surrendered? Are there areas of my life that need repair? Am I experiencing true joy and complete peace?

If you had to respond no to any of these questions, the way to create a positive response is to surrender. Always, the answer is to surrender to God's plan for you. If the One who formed you in your mother's womb and placed the stars in the sky can be trusted with all of creation, then why not trust Him with your life?

You may be inclined to believe that it is too late for you to surrender. You may think that you have made too many mistakes or sinned too grievously. But as the stories in this book prove time after time, life after life, it is never too late to surrender to our Father. He always stands ready to forgive.

God gives each and every one of us unique gifts. If you feel yours have been untapped or dormant, it is because your Creator has been waiting for you to surrender all to Him. When we understand that our very desires have been placed within us by God and that true peace and happiness are found only when we fulfill what He created us to do, only then can we have true peace, joy, and contentment surpassing all understanding.

It is my fervent hope that a desire to pursue God's purpose for you has been sparked in your heart after reading the simple stories of real people in this book. I know that God is able to speak to you, and I know that He is ready to show you the path He has designed for you specifically. It is my prayer that you will find the path of purpose that God intends for you. I know that will happen if you surrender your will to His.

Exciting times lie ahead for all willing to surrender. Life will not be perfect, nor will it be painless. But there is no greater life than the one that follows the path God sets before it. The Path of Surrender is a place of peace within a place of rest. Each of us is born uniquely gifted and talented, and to use our talents and abilities as God intended provides the purpose of our lives.

Few experiences are more profound than finding your place in this life and knowing that it is just a steppingstone to eternity. We matter to God. We can make a difference in the lives of His other children. That is why surrendering to God's plan is so important. The decision is yours now and forever. Our loving Father will not impose Himself on our lives. He gives us a choice.

Today will you choose surrender? If so, I am excited for what God has in store for you and blessed to offer you a simple prayer to begin your journey.

Lord, I surrender my life to You. Take my life and use it as You have designed. I may not understand everything, but I trust You to lead and guide me into all truth. I surrender everything to You right now. Amen.

Your Letter of Surrendering All

Write your own Prayer of Surrender here in the form of a letter. There is not one correct way to do this, but a guideline I suggest is to follow the ABCs:

Ask for God's forgiveness for your sins.

Believe that His Son died on the cross for your sins.

Commit to surrendering your life to His will.

Acknowledgments

I would like to thank my heavenly Father first and foremost for His amazing presence in my life. I cannot imagine living or breathing without Him.

Secondly, I would like to thank my amazing family—first my husband, Marcus, who is my friend, my lover, the father of our children, and my greatest inspiration next to the Lord; also my three fantastic kids, Jonathan, Rachel, and Rebecca, who have brought me the greatest joy a mother could ever experience.

Lastly, a big thanks to my parents, Bill and Sandra Trammell, who raised me with godly values; and my three siblings, Rusty, Kristie, and Lane, along with their families. I love and cherish each one of you.

Notes

Chapter 5

1. Russell Shorto, "Faith at Work," *The New York Times Magazine,* October 31, 2004, http://www.nytimes.com/2004/10/31/ magazine/31FAITH.html?pagewanted=print&position=. Used with permission.

Chapter 6

1. "The Betty Baxter Story," http://www.geocities.com/ bettybaxterstory/story7.html.
2. Suzy A. Richardson, "Tebow's Family Ties," *The Gainesville Sun,* December 6, 2007.

Chapter 7

1. Brian Houston, "The Power of Friendship," http://www2.hillsong .com/brianbobbie/default.asp?pid=1160. Used with permission.

Chapter 8

1. "Oath Taking, Truth Telling, and Remedies in the Business World," 107th Congress House hearings, subcommittee on Commerce, Trade, and Consumer Protection. Testimony by S. Truett Cathy, http://republicans.energycommerce.house.gov/107/ hearings/07262002Hearing681/Smith1153.htm.

Chapter 9

1. P. Bunny Wilson, *Betrayal's Baby* (Pasadena, CA: New Dawn, 1992).

Chapter 10

1. Pat Summerall, *Summerall: On and Off the Air* (Nashville: Thomas Nelson, 2006).

Founded in 1997 by Marcus and Joni Lamb, Daystar Television Network has become the second largest global Christian television network. Daystar operates over fifty television stations in major markets across the United States and is available in every city in America and virtually every country in the world.

Daystar offers the largest selection of programming found in one place, including the most diverse and unique blend of interdenominational and multicultural faith programming from around the world. Known for original, cutting-edge, award-winning programming, Daystar is who today's faith viewers are watching.

The *JONI* show is one of Daystar's most watched original programs, showcasing expert guests with a fresh perspective on health, nutrition, marriage, finance, and other relevant topics for today's viewer. For more on Daystar programming or broadcast times and channels, visit www.Daystar.com.

For more on *Surrender All* or to download Joni's special "Surrender All" music, go to surrenderallbook.com.